Moose Hunting

Moose
Hunting

Calling, Decoying, and Stalking

Dave Kelso
with Peter Fiduccia

Skyhorse Publishing

DEDICATION

To the most influential people in my life.

To my dad, Richard Kelso, thanks for always finding the time when I was growing up to take me hunting and fishing. The trips to camp will always be a big part of my memories. You instilled in me the love for the outdoors that I have today.

To my late great-grandfather Lester who shared his stories of hunting moose in the Skiticook Country. I know you would have been proud of this book.

To my wife, Tracy. Thank you for giving me the encouragement to sit down and write this book. Without your help of reading each chapter, offering suggestions and your constant support, this book would have never been written.

Skyhorse Publishing books may be purchased in bulk at special discounts for sales promotion, corporate gifts, fund-raising, or educational purposes. Special editions can also be created to specifications. For details, contact the Special Sales Department, Skyhorse Publishing, 307 West 36th Street, 11th Floor, New York, NY 10018 or info@skyhorsepublishing.com.

Skyhorse® and Skyhorse Publishing® are registered trademarks of Skyhorse Publishing, Inc.®, a Delaware corporation.

Visit our website at www.skyhorsepublishing.com.

10 9 8 7 6 5 4 3 2 1

Library of Congress Cataloging-in-Publication Data is available on file.

Cover design by Richard Rossiter
Cover photo credit by P. Cody Fiduccia

Print ISBN: 978-1-62873-674-8
Ebook ISBN: 978-1-62914-093-3

Printed in the United States of America

TABLE OF CONTENTS

EDITOR'S NOTE

Moose Hunting was originally published by Woods N' Water Press, Inc., in 2006. For this 2014 edition, most of the original material written by Dave Kelso has been retained, while new information has been provided and other content has been updated and rewritten by Peter Fiduccia. Peter's added and updated material can be found on pages 1–2, 7–10, 113–142, 161–164, and 183–194. Everything has been done to ensure that the updated information is correct to the best of the author's ability.

INTRODUCTION

I still remember seeing my first moose as a child. I was probably eight or nine years old and riding along in my great-grandfather's car on our camp road in T4 R3, Maine, bird hunting. It was not the big bull that we all dream about, but a cow moose, and possibly a yearling cow at that. Gramp stopped the car and I looked at this animal in awe as it stood in the road looking back at us.

"Someday you are going to be able to hunt those animals again," he stated. I remember the rest of the day Gramp telling me stories of his moose hunts, both here in Maine and on his trips to Canada. Being the typical kid, I idolized my great-grandfather and his woodsman abilities. I listened intently as he told me tales about moose from his market-hunting days as well as his leisure-time hunts. Even back then, I could clearly see that the mystique of hunting moose held a very special place in his heart. His eyes turned youthful and his stories turned more animated, than when he regaled us with his deer-hunting stories.

Fast-forward about ten years. It is 1980. The State of Maine is holding its first moose hunt in forty-five years. I am along on a hunt with a friend of mine just as an observer, and to help get the animal out of the woods.

I have to admit it was not the experience that I thought it would be after listening to Gramp's stories. We rounded a bend in the road in our 4x4 pickup truck, and there stood a very respectable bull. A hunter scurried from the stopped truck and proceeded to shoot the moose while it stood in the logging road. Hardly the test of woodsmanship and hunting skill Gramp had led me to believe it took to harvest a trophy bull.

In 1982, Maine held its second moose hunt, and what would turn out to be an annual event in the years to come. I drew a permit myself for the hunt, with my Dad as the sub-permittee.

At the time, the state was divided into moose zones, and my permit was for the area just north of Moosehead Lake in the Lobster Lake region. We stayed at a friend's camp located at Northeast Carry, on the banks of the west branch of the Penobscot River.

Although day one of the hunt was uneventful, day two proved to be much different. Driving in by a logging road at first light, we noticed many fresh moose tracks in the soft gravel. Our friend, Dr. Carl Mayhew of Pittston, Maine, suggested we stop, get out and call.

I was using a tin-can moose call, and after just a few tugs on the string, my adrenaline was running. We actually had three bulls coming from different directions. I can still remember the grunts and the hollow sound of their antlers as they came through the woods, shaking small trees in their

My first moose I ever guided a client to in 1980. The first kill and the stories told by my grandfather made a huge impact on my guiding and how I looked at hunting moose in Maine.

frustration and anger. The same sounds today still make the adrenaline shoot through my system, even though I am not the one pulling the trigger or releasing an arrow onto these huge beasts.

In the years since my first moose hunt, I have been able to guide or accompany friends on each moose hunt in Maine, and witnessed fifty-four of these animals fall to the hunters I was with. Some years, I have had the good fortune, or some might call it luck, to see as many as four moose being harvested during the course of our limited season here in Maine. Some of those moose were the trophy-size bulls that Gramp spoke of with such great passion. Some were smaller bulls that, in the eyes of the permit holder at the time, were just as grand as any fifty-inch animal. To me, each and every time I have been on a moose hunt, it has been an adventure, and I relive all those hunts with a smile on my face.

In 1998, I had the opportunity to watch a video seminar given by Maryo Pepin of Buck Expert Game Calls and Corey Kinney of Straight Arrow Outfitters. These two gentlemen spoke of moose hunting with the passion I had seen in my great-grandfather. I knew that, after watching their presentation, I had to meet these hunters.

Since that fateful day, I am proud to say that I have not only met Maryo and Corey, but have hunted and guided with those exceptional woodsmen and others like them, who share my passion for hunting moose. In the few years that I have known them, I have learned more about moose hunting and moose behavior than I ever thought possible. To them I owe a great debt of gratitude.

I also owe a great debt to my great-grandfather for leaving me the stories of his past hunts and instilling in me the passion of hunting such a great creature.

Moose hunting in Maine has changed since it first started. I feel that now the annual moose hunt is just that, a true hunt. Each year we have seen moose that are harder to hunt. It is much more challenging to get them to come to the calls and decoys. They are truly the animals that Gramp told me about so many years ago.

I hope that in this book you will see that moose hunting is not only a sport, but as Maryo Pepin puts it, "a religion." It's my hope that you may learn something in these pages that will help you, a friend, or a family member to have not only the hunt of a lifetime, but also a story that can be shared with a wide-eyed child who looks up to you and admires your woodsmanship skills.

I have been working on this book for two years. Every time I think it is done, I come up with a trick we have learned and added a new chapter. I finally had to draw a line in the sand and just get it done.

Every good woodsman I have ever known will tell you that there is not a day or hunting trip that goes by that he did not learn something. That is the case with moose hunting as well. I am sure that in the years to come, I will have gained enough knowledge through experience to be able to write another book. Such is hunting.

The information contained in these pages is the comprehensive work of what I have learned, whether on my own or through others. I hope that readers will be able to use the information contained within, and go out and learn something that I may not know. Just remember to pass it along to someone younger, who will carry on the tradition of moose hunting. ■

My Dad and me with two moose taken in two days of hunting at our family camp. My great-grandfather Lester built the camp in the Skiticook area in Aroostook County, Maine.

THE ANIMAL

The moose is the largest member of the deer family. Over the last several decades moose have expanded their geographic range significantly throughout the world. Moose are found throughout most of northern North America, Northern Europe, the Baltic region, Siberia, and even the colder regions of Asia. They have also been transplanted into areas not common to their range including Colorado, Utah, and areas of eastern Canada.

The biggest moose (body weight and antlers) are found in Alaska and the northwestern portions of the Yukon Territory. Mature bulls can weigh in at 1,100 to 1,500 pounds or more. In their southern range (from the 65th to the 40th parallel) moose are smaller than their northern cousins in body and antler size and can weigh 500 to 900 pounds accordingly. However, when it comes to the largest deer, noth-

Alicia Spillane, fourteen, and her moose and me. Alicia dropped the moose with two shots from her 7mm-08 rifle. The bull sported a forty-nine-inch spread. Notice the short points on the palms. This bull was thirteen and one-half years old.

ing is written in stone. If southern moose inhabit areas with extremely nutritious food sources, it is possible for them to equal the weights and antler sizes of their northernmost brethren.

Moose are most often found to inhabit a wide variety of terrains including forests, bogs, cut-overs, and other lands. They instinctively seek out lands that include thick conifers for protection from foul weather and predators. They also inhabit mixed forests that offer good mast and other food sources. Moose are particularly attracted to places dotted with water (lakes ponds, bogs, streams, and swamps). Water provides them with an additional food source from spring to early fall including a variety of water plants. It also provides protection from predators and blood-sucking insects, and during the heat of the summer it is a place to cool off.

NORTH AMERICA MOOSE SUB-SPECIES

All moose belong to one species (*Alces alces linneaus*). Biologists, however, classify moose living in different areas with distinctive taxonomic names. Throughout North America these subspecies include the Alaska-Yukon moose (*Alces alces gigas*, Miller, 1899), the Northwestern moose (*Alces alces andersoni,* Peterson, 1950), the Eastern moose *(Alces alces americanus*, Clinton, 1822), and the Shiras moose (*Alces alces shirasi*, Nelson, 1914).

Although the different subspecies names are used to identify moose living in different regions, not all biologists agree they are necessary. In fact, long-ranging studies have proven that there is little genetic variation between moose living in different regions. Therefore more and more biologists feel there are only two viable subspecies of moose throughout the entire world: the European/West Siberian moose (*Alces alces*, Linnaeus, 1758) and the East Siberian/North American moose (*alces alces americanus*, Clintion, 1822).

THE ALASKA, WESTERN-YUKON, AND NORTHWESTERN BRITISH COLUMBIA MOOSE

Moose living within the areas often referred to as Alaska-Yukon and Northwestern British Columbia are the biggest subspecies of moose in North America. Mature bulls can reach heights of more than eight feet at the shoulders and weights up to 1,500 or more pounds. A fully mature bull can have antlers that are over 70 inches wide and weigh more than fifty pounds. They are the largest wild animal in North America due to the perfuse amount of nutritious and highly digestible plants found within this latitude.

All of my experience has been with the eastern Canadian subspecies. Corey Kinney, of Straight Arrow Outfitters, has hunted moose in Alberta and found that they respond just as well to calls and the methods we employ here in Maine. I have spoken with guides and outfitters from Alaska and they have told me that they use the same hunting methods we use. Maryo has hunted moose in all the Canadian provinces except Saskatchewan, as well as Maine, and finds

This bull taken by Laura Atkins measured fifty-six inches wide. It was aged at three and one-half years old. Genetics and feed played a major role in its antler development.

that all respond to calls and the hunting methods I have outlined in this book. As with other animals, a moose is a moose no matter where you find him.

Moose live on average seven to eight years. They can live well into the teens, but rarely make it past the age of twenty. Here in the northeastern United States, southern Quebec and Ontario, there are very few predators that can kill an adult moose. Calves are susceptible to predation from black bears and coyotes.

In Karen Morris's Bangor office, she has a European mount of a bull moose. Looking at the rack of the bull, you can tell he was on the downward side of his antler development. Karen is quick to point out that he was one of her radio-collared moose from a past research project. The bull met his demise when he walked off a cliff at eighteen years of age. I jokingly said something about Alzheimer's and she laughed, saying it could be possible.

Parasites can inflict major harm upon these huge animals. Brain worm is almost always fatal; lungworm can kill moose, but most often does not unless an individual is severely infected. Karen has found that most moose have lungworm anyway.

3

MOOSE HUNTING

Winter tick is the predominate parasite that takes it toll on the New England moose herd. Although it rarely occurs, ticks have been known to kill calves during years of heavy infestation, and there is no explanation as to why it is worse some years than others. Both Maine and New Hampshire have had epidemic outbreaks of winter tick among their moose herds.

The male moose is capable of breeding at the age of one-and-a-half years, but due to the hierarchy of the species, rarely does a bull breed before he's two and a half. Often, bulls have to be three-and-a-half years old before they're capable of fending off rivals for breeding rights.

The male will develop his first set of antlers when he's one and a half. This is usually just a set of spikes or forks. Palms do not develop until the animal reaches three-and-a-half years, although exceptionally well-fed moose, with the help of genetics, may sport a small set of palmed antlers at the age of two and a half. One year, Corey and I had a hunter that killed a moose with a fifty-inch rack. When the moose was aged, it was found to be only three-and-a-half years old. No doubt genetics played a part in his superior rack.

A moose's antler growth will reach its maximum potential when the animal is five or six years old. When a bull reaches the age of ten to thirteen, his rack size and quality will start to regress. I had a client kill a bull one season that had a forty-eight-inch spread, but very narrow palms. The moose was also very gray in color—not just around the muzzle, but also throughout the entire body. My client received a card from the state that said they had estimated his age through an extracted tooth and found that the bull was fourteen years old. This may have explained his poor-quality rack.

The Maine breeding season starts in late September and continues into mid-October. Maryo, through his captive moose herd, has pinpointed almost to the day on the calendar when breeding activity will occur. His vast hunting experience has proved that moose in the wild are at the same stages as his captive moose. He has also been able to disprove a lot of what old-time moose hunters had been led to believe. I found my interview with him for this book to be highly educational, and it answered many questions for me.

On or around September 10, Maryo expects to hear the first cries of cows going into heat. They will call about ten times in a twenty-four-hour period. While not really in heat, the cows are telling the bulls where they are, and that it will soon be time to breed. In the wild, a bull may go to a cow but keep a distance until she signals that she is ready. As an individual cow's breeding time draws nearer, she will call more often to find her bull.

As estrus draws near, a cow will become intolerant of other cows around her, and if she is with a bull she will chase her rivals off. When Maryo puts two cows to one bull in his breeding pens, the cows will not interact with each other.

Breeding peaks out September 25. Three days prior to this, the cows are constantly agitated with each other. The bull goes to the one he likes best first. If another cow makes a move toward him, the first will try to keep the bull from

A cow moose and calf during the summer in a large beaver flow.

the rival cow by beating up on him. If that fails to keep him in line, she will chase the other cow away.

In a pen situation, the rival cow will just stay on the opposite end of the enclosure from the pair. If she starts giving her cow-in-heat call, the cow with the bull will match those calls in duration, adding more agitation. Her determination to keep the bull away from the competition will increase as well.

The day the first cow is ready to breed, she does not make a sound; she stands waiting for the bull to make his move, but she will keep her rival at bay, away from her man of choice. The other cow, calling in jealousy, will become very loud and extremely agitated.

Maryo has video footage of cows and bulls going through the mating ritual—a penned pair and a wild pair—and there is another rival cow present in both situations. If not for the fact that the wild pair was filmed at night, and the bull is larger, you would swear that you were watching the same ritual. The procedure is almost identical.

When the moose finally mate, it happens very fast. He is on her, then off, and it is done. The cow may let the bull mount her more than once, but when she has had enough, she makes it perfectly clear that she no longer wants his company and will do whatever it takes to drive him off.

It is at this point that the bull becomes very aggressive. This is the stage a bull reaches what we refer to as being "Drooling Stupid." He wants to fight. He has no tolerance for another bull or the sight of another bull. Maryo has to put up screens between the pens to keep the peace or the bulls will try to fight even with the chain link fence between them.

The bull will breed with the other cow in the pen as soon as she is ready. If her time has gone past, she will come back into heat in twenty days and the ritual will start between those two. Should the first cow not be pregnant, she will come back into heat as well. Each cow will come into heat three times, and occasionally more, until she is impregnated.

Cows continue to breed all their lives as long as they are well fed and in good physical shape. Karen and her research team examined a cow taken during a Maine hunting season that was still lactating at eighteen years of age.

Cow moose still show up as barren or without calves, and cows that are not lactating are taken each hunting season. Many cows are seen with no calves present. Maryo, who has done research on this, has had a startling revelation: Once a cow chooses to accept a bull for breeding, she only wants to breed with that bull in the future years!

He has placed a cow in a pen with a bull that she never mated with, although she mated with another bull in years past, and found that the cow refused to accept the stranger. If she can see the bull that she has bred with before, she will stare at him through the fence. Maryo has seen cases where a cow separated from her bull of choice did not even come into heat. When he moved that cow into the pen with her chosen, she immediately came into heat, mated, and became pregnant. Maryo feels that this is why we see cows that appear to be healthy, and yet have no offspring. Eventually, once the cow realizes that she will not be able to find her past lover, she will choose another bull, but it may take her an entire year to realize this.

Over all my fifty years of hunting ruminant mammals throughout North America, I have never seen any other estrus females that compromise the family of Cervidae (deer) act as audacious, or what could also be accurately described as somewhat bawdy, as a cow moose. They are without a doubt the Jane Mansfield sex symbols of the deer world. A mature cow moose is not shy about coming on strong to a bull. Unlike other female deer of different species, when a cow moose is ready to mate, she isn't about to wait for the bull to initiate romance. Without much regard for being "ladylike," a cow moose will make long moaning grunts and groans announcing to all bull moose within hearing distance that she is ready to meet all suitors. When a bull does arrive, grunting, swaying his rack from side to side, and drooling from the mouth, the cow is not introverted about repeatedly rubbing her body against his while she utters her most seductive lamenting vocalizations. She desires male attention, and to make her intentions perfectly clear, she vocalizes and makes body contact with a bull, assuring him of her cravings.

It is exactly this behavior that warrants one of the most productive and consistently successful moose-hunting strategies when moose hunting—calling. Because most moose habitat is vast and thickly wooded terrain, finding a mate takes some doing. So during the rut, both cows and bulls are on the constant move over bogs and through impenetrable Tuckamore, thick timberlands, swamps, mountainous terrain, and vast open bogs, mewing, grunting, bellowing, and gutturalizing to each other. During the rut, the woods and waters that moose inhabit become alive with vocalizations.

No matter what part of North America a hunter stalks moose, during the rut, knowing how to use a moose call correctly will get results. During the breeding season bull moose are much more cantankerous than whitetail deer, mule deer, caribou, and even the belligerent bull elk. During the rut, a mature bull is not to be trifled with. He is often in a murderous mood and will stomp, gore, and otherwise put out of commission anything he interprets as a threat, or worse, what he thinks is a competitor for his estrus cow.

Bulls spend their rutting days scent urinating—the perfume of the rut. A week or two before cows come into estrus and are ready to breed, bulls begin to paw shallow depressions in the ground with the front hooves. The hole may be only a few inches deep, but on some occasions it can be over a foot deep. It can also vary in its size as well, from just a few feet long to more than a half dozen feet in length. Bulls also use the massive antlers to dispatch and fling any unwanted vegetation from the area as well. Once the depression suits the bull fancy, and a few mock urinating sessions, he will squat over the hollow he has made and begin to actually deposit what seems to be an unending amount of urine into the hole.

Corey Kinney and I interact with a cow at the research center. The cow has one eye trained on me and the other on Corey. Notice the ears as well—one is pointed toward me and the other is focused in on Corey.

Once he deposits an ample amount of urine into the depression it will muddy up the soil. At this point, they bull will lie down in the shallow pit and begin to roll his entire body back and forth until he is satisfied he has covered most of it in his stinking pee, which is cologne to cow moose. Bulls, like elk, will make several of these "wallows" to bathe in during the rut.

Amazingly, and again unlike the more reserved females within the family of Cervidae (deer), the cow moose is not only drawn to the stench of the bull's urine, but she will often use it to roll around in as well, whether the bull is lying in it or not! Interestingly, the bull will run the cow out of the wallow. Not so much to chase her away, but rather to give him more time to stink himself up with his "Urine de Pee." By deeply soaking themselves with their urine, bulls instinctively know the pungent odor will naturally draw cows from near and far to them. The odor invites females to rub and snuggle close to them in order to get the bull's "stank" on themselves, which stimulates them into estrus more quickly. Ah, the ritual of the moose rut runs deep and smelly.

In a research study that took place in Denali National Park in Alaska in the mid-eighties, researcher Dale Miquelle and his team from the University of Idaho made interesting behavioral observations of bulls making wallows over a three-year period. What they discovered was that only mature bulls took part in this type of "scent urine" behavior. The research team believed that the urine odor of immature bulls simply wasn't as powerful as was the urine of mature bull moose.

The team also documented that immature bulls would often bathe in the urine left in the wallows made by mature bulls, but only when the older bulls weren't around, in hopes the odor of the older bulls would attract cows. When a mature bull saw this behavior he immediately and aggressively chased the immature bull from his wallow. Females were also noticed to compete with each other to roll in the wallow as well and often rubbed their bodies against the bodies of the mature males. This urine scent behavior generally took place about two weeks prior to when cows would actually accept bulls to breed them. Miquelle and his research team's conclusion of scent urination behavior was that it was most likely used to stimulate ovulation in cow moose.

As I have often mentioned in my deer-hunting seminars, male deer all measure up their opponents carefully before they get into an all-out brawl. It is Mother Nature's way of protecting them from opening themselves up to an abundance of serious or fatal injuries. This is particularly the case for the larger-bodied moose, caribou, and elk. Before engaging their antlers, moose and other male deer often use boxing tactics similar to human fighters who are about to get into a fistfight. The scuffle usually begins with trash talking. In the world of the moose, that means the bull will grunt, croak, and groan to try and "talk" his opponent out of actual antler and body contact.

If that fails, a bull will quickly throw in some aggressive body language. He begins by lifting his head high to show off the size of his antlers. Then he pins both ears back, raises the hair on his mane, and begins to stiff leg around his opponent. Anyone who has hunted moose knows this ritual also includes the bull slowly swaying his antlers from side to side menacingly in order to let his opponent get a good look as his impressive head gear. The body language ritual also includes staring, ripping up vegetation, thrashing brush, and knocking the snot out of nearby sapling trees. This is all done to warn to the opposing bull that he should back down post-haste. Sometimes the rituals last for short periods of time, but other times they last for hours and, in rare cases, even days depending on the two bulls engaging in this type of rutting behavior.

While a majority of moose breeding activity takes place from late September to early October in most regions, breeding can occur well into November when late-cycling cows come into estrus. I have seen bulls called in by outfitters (particularly in Newfoundland) using seductive cow calls as late as December! Once a bull's testosterone levels begin to wane, they usually deplete quickly. Once that occurs a bull moose will generally drop his antlers soon thereafter; most bulls shed their antlers around January. By late March mature bulls are already beginning to grow their velvet. Within a few short months the velvet reaches the massive proportions common to male moose, and by late August or early September it is shed and polished and ready to do battle during the moose rut once again.

MOOSE ANTLERS

Hunters are mesmerized by antlers, and when it comes to a bull moose's antlers, they are particularly spellbound by the huge mass of bone atop a bull's head! It is a little known fact, however, that a bull's antlers are not any larger than other male deer's antlers like elk, caribou, and mule and white-tailed deer. Relative to body size, moose antler mass is about equal to other male deer species. With that said, today's moose still grow the largest antlers in the world. As mentioned earlier, the Alaskan-Yukon moose grow the most antlers in the least amount of time. The can grow about ninety to a hundred pounds of antlers in approximately three months!

Dominant bulls killed during the hunting season, or meeting their demise from other circumstances, may leave a cow wandering the entire breeding season looking for her mate. She might go through all three heats, and occasionally a fourth, and still not be bred. The next breeding season, she will normally take another male as her partner.

This may explain why we often see areas that, year after year, produce good moose hunting; they are breeding areas. Cows know that the dominant bulls they have chosen in the past are going to be in a particular area, and they flock to it. Young bulls or even bulls that are not dominant also show up there because of the cows.

Once the dominant bull is missing from the area, the younger competing bulls will eventually be able to breed with the available cows. This sets up a scenario where you may have several cows that are all breeding with different bulls, not necessarily the dominant bull. Now you have a situation where bulls and cows return to a particular place for breeding because they know it is where they found their past lovers hanging out—and that makes for a great hunting ground.

The gestation period for moose is approximately seven months. Calves are born from May on into June, and cows that don't find their mates until they're into the third heat may not calf until July. A cow will have one to two calves, depending on her age and nutritional condition, and a calf will stay with its mom until shortly before the next calving season, at which time the cow will chase her young away.

The cow moose is highly aggressive when it comes to protecting her offspring. I have learned through experience to give cows with calves a wide berth. Do not get between a cow and her calf and then surprise her, because you will not like the outcome, as I learned the hard way. Maryo has observed this trait at the research center as well.

Because the moose has a very sensitive nose, I take greater care to keep my moose-hunting clothes scent free than I do with my deer-hunting attire. I have had moose scent me and spook when I thought everything was perfect. Yet while deer hunting, I have actually touched a deer that walked by me without smelling me. I am still waiting to be able to get that close to moose.

The moose also has those two big radar dishes located on top of its head, the ears. I refer to their ears as radar because of the animal's ability to move each ear independently, which allows them to better pinpoint the exact direction and location of sounds. I am always amazed at the distances over which I have been able to get a moose to respond to my calls. Just to level up the playing field, I have gone to using hearing enhancement equipment. Even on windy days, when I haven't been able to hear anything but the trees swaying, I have had moose show up when I call.

Maryo is right in his observation that you cannot sneak up on a moose. A hunter's best chance at stalking a moose is to walk through a hunting area sounding like another moose. Moose are used to hearing others of their kind, but they will flee if they detect something coming in on them quietly.

The moose's eyesight is its one weakness. They can only see in focus for a distance of ten to fifteen feet—the average would be closer to twelve feet—relying on shape, movement and color, to a degree, to make identification.

Maryo, through his research, has found that on windless days, the right movements from a hunter will pique the curiosity of a moose and make him come closer. On the other hand, moving through an area like a man will cause moose to beat feet. The moose utilizes his hearing much more on windy days; when everything around him is swaying from side to side, he has a hard time detecting individual objects moving about.

MOOSE HUNTING

The moose sees in black and white, as other large mammals do. However, after observing these animals over the years, I think that their color perception is a little more defined than that of whitetail deer. I have had numerous deer not spot me if I am standing perfectly still, although I'm wearing a full blaze-orange jacket and hat. I had one buck that walked within twelve feet of me while I stood on a hardwood ridge, with nothing around me whatsoever to conceal or break my outline.

I once had a doe deer walk all around me, as close as fifteen feet, while I was dressed in fluorescent orange and calling to her. I only used the call when her head was behind a tree, and she would look in my direction, but not right at me. Her eyes appeared to be looking to the right and to the left of my location. She was continuously stomping her feet and snorting, but I remained perfectly still and she could not see me. I am sure she smelled me as she walked around, yet she would not run off, as she could not actually detect any movement. This game went on for over thirty minutes. She finally saw me when I raised my gun to shoot a buck that had come into see what all the commotion was about.

Moose always seem to stare right at any small blotch of orange that does not look right in its world. Even if the hunter does not move, they zero in on the alien color; even if I am using the call and standing some distance away from the hunter, a moose will always focus on the orange hat first as it comes into view, as I have found through my own field testing. My clients and I might wear masks to obscure our faces, but if we're wearing orange hats, a moose will instantly zero in on the hats.

I recommend that, when possible, hunters wear the minimum amount of orange required by law. If you have to wear blaze orange, then do what you can through the use of existing vegetation and trees to keep out of the moose's direct sight. Knowing that orange is a beacon to these animals, I have gone so far as to strategically place fir boughs around my hunters to cover their colored gear as much as possible.

Maryo and I had a lengthy discussion on this issue, and he has found the same to be true, having tested the eyesight of moose, deer, and caribou. He told me that deer are the worst at distinguishing color. Moose are not far behind, but they do see orange and some other non-natural colors much better. Caribou have possibly the best eyesight when it comes to distinguishing color.

The moose is also able to move each eye independently of the other, and if you ever see this up close, you'll have all you can do not to laugh. It will appear as if he is cockeyed, watching you and trying to see something else off to the side.

I have had a moose look at me with a decoy using one eye while his other eye was looking to the left at a cameraman. The cameraman was at a ninety-degree angle to the moose, I was a distance of fifteen feet from away, and I could see the bull's eyes perfectly. I had all I could do to keep from busting out laughing.

I am feeding a cow moose at the Buck Expert Research center.

Moose use a variety of habitats, depending on the time of year. Early spring finds them wandering all about, and they will often be seen in the hardwoods feeding after a hard winter on the first new tips of growth. They are also very prone to frequent roadsides—again getting the first new-generation tips, and attracted to salt that is left on the roads during the winter.

As the summer progresses, moose will use waterways more. They are especially fond of water-lily bulbs and roots, and will also utilize cattails for food, eating the stalk and root. The water keeps them cool on hot days, and they will actually lay down in it to escape the flies and other biting insects.

When breeding season rolls around, moose shift into the breeding areas I spoke of, which often have a waterway of one type or another and are usually not too far from a stand of hardwoods. Most often during the rut, the moose are still prone to be near the water, since the weather is still warm and many aquatic plants are still available to them.

Once the post-rut season rolls around, the moose will be putting on the feed bags for the coming winter. Maryo has found that bulls lose as much as two hundred pounds during the rutting period in a pen environment, and bulls in the wild may lose even more weight. The bulls want to gain back all the bulk they lost chasing cows during the rut, while the cows, now pregnant, want to put on all the fat they can, knowing they are eating for two or three now. Often at this time of year, you will find the moose have moved to hardwood ridges and river bottoms made up of popular and other hardwood species. Regenerating cuts with lots of red maples will draw them in as well.

Winter finds the moose moving through the hardwoods. Being long legged, they do not have the difficulty that whitetail deer face coping with snow, but if the snow does become a burden—building to more than three feet high—moose will yard up as deer do. Crusty snow will also have an effect on them, and under such conditions, moose will seek out the overhead canopy of spruce or other softwood growth, the same as whitetails.

Zoos and other research facilities have come to Maryo, who has had a captive herd of moose since 1995, for his expertise on keeping the animals alive and healthy in captivity. He has done considerable research on a moose's diet, and learned that they not only switch over to various foods because of availability, but also because they need the nutrients provided by particular plants.

During the winter months, an adult moose may consume forty-four pounds of fir tips, twenty pounds of hardwood tips and bark, and Maryo feeds them an additional fifteen pounds of a pellet of his own making to provide some vitamins. The fir tips, while not high in nutrition, contain an oil that Maryo feels is essential in the metabolism of the moose to produce body heat. Zookeepers who have consulted him always seem to have a problem keeping the moose healthy during the winter. After putting them on a high fir-tip diet, their health turned right around.

During the summer months, the amount of food the moose are fed is cut in half and the fir tips are excluded from the diet. Nursing cows will eat a little more to support their milk-production requirements.

Due to Maryo's urine-collection operation and his goals to provide one hundred percent natural urine, he does not feed his animals anything but natural foods during the collection periods, striving to produce urine that matches what would be found in the wild.

Karen Morris, whose research has also shown that moose eat many different foods throughout year, discovered that there is one item they absolutely devour. She said that during her radio-collared moose study, she came upon a feeding area where the vegetation had been eaten so far down to the ground, it took her a while to determine what the plant was. After an afternoon of searching, she learned the moose's favorite food was mountain ash. I always knew that black bear would eat this shrub, but finding out that it's a moose favorite was a surprise to me.

Moose all vary when it comes to a defined home range. The radio-collar research done in Maine and New Hampshire shows that they have no set limits, unlike whitetail deer. Karen told me her studies have shown that moose will utilize an area of eight to twelve square miles, varying with the time of year and food availability. She had one cow moose that lived in a substantially smaller area than that, but she has also seen a bull travel even farther during the rut.

Every fall, New England newspapers have reports of moose that show up in the oddest places, such as downtown Bangor and Portland, Maine. The outskirts of Boston and Manchester, New Hampshire, are not without their odd moose stories as well. Most of these news accounts are of young bulls that have most likely been pushed from an area by a more dominant bull. Following their powerful urge to breed, they will wander aimlessly looking for an area that contains females and no competition, skewing the defined home-range average.

Karen Morris has done a commendable job in managing the Maine moose herd, and Maine often participates in the informal but extremely useful Northeast Moose Study Group, sharing information gleaned through Karen's research among the various states and provinces, since funding shortages often make information sharing just about the only way many fish and wildlife agencies can stay abreast of current trends in managing moose.

Karen hopes that in the future more money can be set aside for certain studies. In particular, she would like to see more research done on young-of-the-year survival rates, so important to the continuation of the sport of moose hunting. She also hopes that in the future, Maine and other states will stay with consistent hunting-season dates. This not only helps hunters pattern moose from year to year, but also gives researchers a better baseline for information gathered by hunters.

During the extensive timber clear-cutting that took place in the '80s moose never caught up to the habitat availability, but Karen sees a steady future for the Maine moose herd. Now that timber companies have reduced the amount of clear-cuts and gone to more selective cuts due to the healthy forests, Maine moose still have an abundance of feed. Karen feels that her goal—to have a population that will utilize sixty percent of the carrying capacity of the available habitat—may or may not be attainable. The winter tick outbreak from time to time could keep the moose herd in check.

Along with the limited hunting, we may be looking at the height of our eastern moose herd. Karen did state that even if hunting were banned again in hopes of attaining the desired population levels, there is no guarantee that would occur. Maine is on the southern fringe of moose habitat, and because of that geographic location, its moose are more susceptible to parasites and viruses. Currently, she feels the moose herd is healthy and can withstand the present level of hunting.

Karen did state that should we ever again see the extensive clear-cuts that we saw back in the '80s due to the spruce budworm outbreak, there could be another spike in moose population numbers. Since no one can predict a spruce budworm outbreak, we have no way of knowing if it will ever happen again.

Her biggest problem, however, seems to be balancing the number of moose with how large a herd the public is willing to tolerate in high human-population areas. An increase in the number of moose-car collisions often results in a pub-lic outcry to reduce the herd in a particular area.

Karen is the "biologist's biologist" in my opinion, after having interviewed her. When I questioned her on the decline of the moose herd in Maine back in the early 1900s, she said that without having all the biological data available from that time period, we may never be sure what decimated the population. Yet she feels that from what she knows now, and early accounts written by biologists of the day, over-the-counter licenses, along with unregulated hunting, was the downfall of the herd. That should not happen today, and it is doubtful it ever will.

Maryo's research continues on, geared more to the hunter, but he does have a lot to share with fish and wildlife departments throughout the northeastern United States and Canada, and he has an interesting theory concerning moose populations along the Maine-Quebec border.

Quebec's border region, near Maine, has a high human-population density as well as a substantial moose population. Many Canadian hunters utilize this area, and their success rate with moose in the region has increased over the years. Many bulls are killed along the border corridor, and Quebec officials thought the rate might be too high.

Maryo stated that of the bulls killed there, not many appear to be dominant animals. Lots of forty-inch-and-under bulls in the three-and-a-half-year age group are taken annually, as this area of Quebec only allows the harvesting of bulls and calves. A winter herd survey indicated that there was an overabun-dance of cows compared to bulls.

When questioned by Quebec biologists about the bulls killed seven to ten miles from the border, Maryo had a theory: He suggested that many of those young bulls were coming from Maine, displaced by larger, more-dominant bulls and lured across the border area because of all the cows available. They breed and then return to the other side of the border, where the habitat is predominantly commercial forest, not farmland as it is on the Quebec side.

The bulls that are showing up a distance from the border are still drawn by cows. A bull hears one cow a mile from the border and he tends to her; he hears another cow farther inland and he goes to her. This can occur over and over, which means bulls can conceivably roam several miles inside of Quebec.

The whole scenario that Maryo lays out makes sense, and maybe someday Maine and Quebec will work on a joint radio-collar study to determine if this is the case. ■

HUNTING METHODS

Methods for hunting moose are not any different than hunting other members of the deer family. Many different tactics will work at different times, depending on the season and the seasonal activity of the moose. I have hunted moose about every way possible and have had success with all of them.

More often than not, a hunter will employ a couple of the different methods combined in one hunt. For example, still-hunting can be combined with the use of calling, or stand hunting can be done over a baited area. Most all of these methods outlined work well with each other as well as alone.

ROAD HUNTING

Back in the early 1980s, when we started hunting moose in Maine after a forty-five-year closed season, many moose were easily taken by simply riding the logging roads. All a hunter had to do was wait for a moose to be spotted on or near the road, and shoot it. Even after twenty-three years, many hunters still opt

An example of a typical clear-cut that was once so abundant back in the 1980s.

for this method because of its ease, and because it allows them to cover lots of ground each day.

However, I have seen the success rate of hunters and guides using this method drop over the years. Many hunters are still taking moose by road hunting; they are just not taking trophy bulls with any consistency. In the 1980s, there were some factors that I think played into making road hunting a successful hunting method.

First off, moose had not been hunted for quite some time, and I believe that the evolutionary process took its toll, eroding the animal's natural wariness. I still remember the stories my great-grandfather told me. To him, the moose was a much tougher animal to hunt than a whitetail deer. He reveled in the idea of being able to fool a moose, and seemed much prouder of the fact he had killed a small bull moose than he was about any of the two hundred-pound bucks he had taken.

I found that during the first few years of our Maine moose hunt, moose simply stood around and watched, probably out of curiosity, as hunters scrambled from a truck and loaded guns. Today, very few of the larger bulls are simply standing around waiting to be shot. Evolution has come full circle, and now I can appreciate Gramp's stories of the moose's wariness.

The second factor that I think played an important role in making road hunting particularly attractive was the vast clear-cuts Maine had in 1980s. The woods were recovering from a severe infestation of the spruce budworm—the larval stage of a moth that caused untold devastation to our commercial forests. With the softwood trees being literally eaten alive and left to die, land managers had no choice but to go into these devastated areas and harvest the affected trees. This caused the massive clear-cuts that dotted our landscape back then.

The clear-cuts made for excellent soil to be rejuvenated with small hardwood browse, such as the maple and poplar trees that moose feed on. This created a magnet effect. Moose were drawn out into the open to feed, and then bedded down in the open, with no fear of man. A moose is no different from you or me; he does not want to work or travel any farther than he has to in order to survive. Hey, put a refrigerator next to a man's easy chair and he is not going to leave it without good reason. Moose are the same.

With the huge clear-cuts available to hunters and easy access via the maintained logging roads, moose hunting in Maine was looked at as way to fill the freezer quickly. Not much of a hunt, if you ask me.

Couple these two factors with the moose's poor eyesight, and you can see why road-hunting for moose became the accepted form here in Maine. Today, road hunting in states where it is legal can still be effective at certain times.

Road-hunters need to look for areas with good visibility. Roads that are grown in tight with alders and other thickly bunched trees are not going to be good. Where clear-cut logging practices are still in use, seek them out as well as the wider secondary logging roads.

There are three basic scenarios that come into play while road hunting. The first one is that the moose is spotted standing in the road. The truck is stopped and the hunter exits the vehicle. If using a clip-loaded weapon, he simply slips the clip into the weapon, chambers a round, takes aim, and fires.

While the hunter is loading the gun, depending on his excitability level, many things are going to happen, and I think, in my experience, I have seen it all. Believe me, depending on the hunter's skill, there is going to be some major movement going on. So the hunter will need to minimize as much movement as possible.

Have the shooter keep the vehicle door open and stand behind it; it will hide a lot of movement from the moose. As I said earlier, if using a clip-fed weapon, slide the clip in and chamber a round. If the weapon uses rounds that must be thumbed into the magazine, make sure the shooter only takes the time to thumb two rounds.

This young bull with developing antlers is attracted to a roadside salt run-off.

This can be done efficiently, as opposed to trying to thumb a complete magazine full into the gun. At best you may only have the opportunity to fire two rounds anyway. Adrenaline will be flowing at this point, so keeping the human error factor to a minimum is a must for a successful road-hunt.

Guide Dan Glidden of Ashland, Maine, brought a neat little trick to my attention during a hunt in the northern part of that state. One morning, under very windy conditions, he had set up and called with a hunter. Nothing happened, so Dan decided to move on to his next spot. After getting in the truck and traveling a very short distance, a bull was spotted in the road and more than likely, coming to Dan's call. The moose, being somewhat stymied at seeing a truck and not another moose, stood in the road and looked at the vehicle.

Dan's hunter exited the truck, keeping the door open as he'd been instructed to do, turned his back to the moose and loaded his weapon. At one point he looked at Dan and asked, "Is he still there?" Dan replied that he was. The hunter took a deep breath and turned, saw his target, took aim, and fired. The moose pretty much died in the road making Dan's work easy.

This hunter knew full well that he might get overly excited, recognizing his excitability limits, and he did not want to be looking at the animal while he was trying to do something as intricate as thumbing rounds into his weapon's magazine.

I have since instructed my hunters to face away from the moose while loading a weapon and it has worked well. I would highly recommend this technique to anyone else who might have a small excitability problem. Hey, we're all human and there's nothing wrong with getting excited about the chance to bag such a magnificent animal.

The next common scenario is a moose that is spotted on the side of the road as you are driving by. This calls for a great deal of composure from both the person who spots the moose and the driver of the vehicle, although sometimes composure and moose hunting cannot be used in the same sentence.

When someone in a vehicle spots a moose, he or she should not say anything to anyone, just allow the vehicle to keep moving at the same speed and in the same direction to minimize everyone's excited reaction. Drive past the moose and keep on moving far enough beyond the site that you cannot see it and you're convinced that it cannot see you. It might be one hundred feet or one hundred yards, depending on the landscape. Once you feel you are a safe distance away, stop the vehicle, have the hunter get out and load his weapon.

Now, to cut down on the amount of movement, only the person who saw the moose and the hunter should get out and walk back to where the animal was spotted. There is no need to take the entire hunting party.

Chances are the moose will have moved, so be on the lookout for it. The moose may have come closer to the road or walked farther back into the woods. Each moose has its own agenda and is going to react differently.

Hopefully, you will have the moose standing somewhere near where it was first sighted and the hunter will be able to get a shot off. If the moose is gone and nowhere to be found, chalk it up to an educated moose and move on. You may be able to come back another day and work him with a call, but now is not the time. He knows what you are and the danger you represent to his well-being.

Another scenario that often happens while road hunting: You are driving along and you spot a moose running; makes no difference whether it is in the road or off to the side. It does not like what it hears and sees, and it's running. This scenario can go so many different ways. Let's take it from the top.

The moose is running down the road in front of the vehicle and cuts off to the side. My first instinct is to stop and hope the moose will stop and look back, a seemingly common trait among most of the deer family. I have trained myself to avoid this instinct and to keep driving at the same speed as when I saw the moose. Let him cut off to the side, and continue to drive by as if you are no threat to him.

Moose are very accustomed to logging trucks, heavy equipment, and other disinterested parties traveling through their range. He may very well stop and want to continue on the pre-planned path that you interrupted. Drive past him far enough and then come walking back. You may very well find him where you last saw him.

Another scenario might go like this: The moose is spotted on the side of the road in a cut or other small opening. He is more than likely already looking at your vehicle. Keep driving at the same speed, do not stop, and do not put on the brakes. It is tough and no one knows that more than me, having done it countless times. Just drive well past the animal, and by well past, I mean at least a quarter of a mile; half a mile may be better. Pull your vehicle to the side of the road and then walk back looking for the animal.

Chances are that if he has spotted you and is looking at you, he's wondering what you're up to. Stop right in front of him and he will more than likely bolt, and you will never see him again. Drive by him and he may dismiss you as one of the vehicles that he sees all year, due to logging. I have done this many times and found the bull standing pretty much where I left him. Other times I have not driven far enough past, and the moose, deciding that I represented some sort of threat, took off for safer ground. It is a judgment call on your part.

Having spent many hours in the woods while both hunting moose and observing them during other outdoor activities, I can tell you that you need to be able to read the moose when you first spot it. But be advised that you are not going to read the animal correctly every time. There are many "between-the-lines" clues that you need to be looking for—more than I could possibly cover in this book. Experience with live animals will be your best teacher. The more time you can spend searching out these animals and noting their behavior, the better a hunter you will become.

STILL-HUNTING

Still-hunting for moose is not much different than still-hunting for other members of the deer family, and much of the material written in the countless books about whitetail hunting can also be applied to moose—although the moose tends to stand out much better due to its coloring and size. Other than that, you just need to be in an area that holds a good population of them.

During years when our Maine moose season has fallen outside of the rut and calling has not been a major factor, still-hunting has proven to be very effective and hunters should not overlook this method. The key is to get into areas where you know moose live, and have a back-up plan for those times when they do not respond to calls readily.

My own experiences still-hunting for moose duplicates my experience with whitetails: Get into an area that holds your quarry. Go slow. Look over everything that is not in the normal order of Mother Nature's vertical patterns, and pay close attention to horizontal shapes. Also, with moose, take particular note of black stump-like forms. Look over any root formations that may have been created when a tree blew over in a windstorm. Often these uprooted trees tear away a lot of topsoil and expose the much cooler under-soil. In warm weather, a moose will bed down in damp blackened earth to let the moisture help him cool off.

In the 1980s, many moose were spotted laying in the shade of uprooted trees in the huge clear-cuts that were abundant back then. Not only did these moose feel cooler because of the soil composition, but also, I believe, they felt safe due to the shadows of the root mass.

At one time, while still-hunting for moose, I would go as quietly as I would for whitetails. Having spent considerable time with Corey and Maryo, and factoring in my own observations, I have changed my opinion about that.

Moose that are moving through the woods tend to make a lot of noise when they are relaxed and everything in their surroundings seems normal. You will hear the cracking of brush as they walk along. With a bull, you will hear his antlers scraping on the trees and bushes as he walks along feeding.

Whenever I have to resort to still-hunting, I walk through the woods as a moose would. I spend more of my time looking for moose than I do worrying about where I am stepping. Also, if I am not the one who has to tote a gun along, then I have my raking antler with me and I will scrape and bang it on trees as I walk. All I want to do is sound like a moose to any other moose that may be in the area.

If, through your scouting, you find an area that has many beds, consider it a good bet for still-hunting. Tall grass and scattered bushes will most likely be the normal vegetation. Hunt through the area slowly and watch for movement in the vegetation. It may not be the wind.

With large areas of tall grass, such as in a clear-cut or a heath, look for places that are dark in color and low to the ground. Scrutinize these closely with your binoculars and pay close attention to any branch or stick rising above the grass. More than one bull moose has been spotted because a portion of his antlers showed above the surrounding vegetation.

Look for older clear-cuts or selective cuts that have grown up in small soft-wood trees mixed with maples and other moose feed. Moose, being lazy, will get a belly full to eat and then just lay down where the mood suits them. You could spend all day walking slowly through these areas, which can be effective, but will take up a lot of your time.

I prefer to find a high point overlooking likely bedding areas. This can be a hill or it may be as simple as the pushed up dirt banking formed when the road was built. In many cuts an old pile of pulpwood will be left behind. Once I get into position on high ground, I make a couple of bull grunts. If a moose is sleeping out in this area you may not be able to detect his presence until he stands up to see what is going on. If you lack the ability to successfully duplicate the bull grunt or are hunting an area that receives a lot of pressure from other moose callers try simply snapping a stick or two over your knee. The loud crack of the breaking stick is going to sound like another moose moving through the area. This is more than enough to get a moose to stand up and show himself. Just do not over do the stick breaking. One or two loud snaps will get a moose to stand up and look around with out putting him on alert.

When moving into one of these bedding areas, play the wind. I cannot stress this enough. Keep the wind into your face or at least perpendicular to the suspected location of a bedding moose. Nothing is going to make him bolt faster than your scent hitting him in the nose.

On more than one occasion during deer season I have worked through a cut over area with the wind in my favor and spotted nothing. After having walked by a bedded moose my scent drifted back to him. The moose have left with a crash and blur of antlers and moose butt. No doubt had I made some noise during my still hunt I would have made him stand and show himself. But since I was not hunting moose it was just another chance to observe their behavior.

CANOE HUNTING

Hunting from a canoe has to be the epitome of moose hunting, as close to a perfect way to hunt such a noble creature as there could ever be. The thought of it conjures up images of huge bulls standing on the banks of small ponds or in river backwaters feeding on water-lily roots.

If you decide to hunt moose from a canoe, look at it as if you were still-hunting. First make sure the waterway you plan on hunting has moose along it. I would hesitate to canoe a lengthy river that only has one small section of moose habitat. Your time might be better spent using a different method.

You can use calling as your primary way to bring moose to you, or you can rely on the animal's need to feed to bring them out. Depending on the time of the season, you will see moose either way.

At times, hunters in kayaks slip into areas more quietly than on foot. A canoe makes transportation of the moose easier.

MOOSE HUNTING

Your main concern when you are canoe hunting is to stay quiet. Any noise you make from a canoe is going to be an unnatural in the moose's environment, which is why I do not recommend using an aluminum canoe as a hunting platform. Aluminum banging into rocks and sliding over logs is quite noisy, so a modern canoe made of Royalex or fiberglass, or a traditional canoe made of cedar and glass, is your best bet. Even with canoes made of these materials, I suggest that you place a piece of carpeting on the inside bottom of the craft to muffle the sound of adjusting your feet or anything that you may drop. The carpeting will also create one more layer of insulation between you and the cold water, and that will help keep your feet warmer.

If you are maneuvering your canoe with a pick pole rather than a paddle, use the wood end of the pole rather than the end with the metal pick. When it strikes rocks on a river bottom, the wood will sound more like a moose's hoof than the clickety-clack of the metal end jabbing on stone.

If you are using a paddle for propulsion, get yourself a quality wooden one. There aren't too many good composite paddles on the market. Not only will the wood paddle be quieter in the water, but you can also use it to rattle overhanging alders to simulate a moose raking his antlers. Many of the composite paddles just sound way too tinny when rattled that way.

Traveling down a stream or river or slowly paddling a lakeshore is the preferred method of canoe hunting. Move along slowly, especially when you are in a known feeding area—and I cannot stress how slow, slow is. At times moving with the current is going to be too fast!

Often, in the early morning hours when sound travels best, you may be able to hear a moose up to a half-mile or more from where you are. Listen closely enough and you'll get an idea about his line of travel, and hear where you might need to be to head him off.

Corey Kinney did a canoe hunt one year on the Allagash River. Before daylight, he and his hunter launched their canoe at Bissonette Bridge, just below Churchill Dam. First light found them just upstream of Umsaskis Lake, adjacent to the big heaths that surround the south end of the lake.

Both Corey and the hunter could hear a moose in the alder swale that borders the heaths. His antlers could be heard scrapping the alder and poplar trees. Once in a while, they could hear a branch snap under the weight of the moose. It was late in the season, post rut, and no amount of calling would interest the bull. He just kept feeding and paying no attention to the calls.

Corey made the decision to go after it by still-hunting. He and the hunter beached the canoe, got a line on the moose's direction of travel, and proceeded to attempt to cut it off. The hunter was trying not to make any noise, and Corey finally told him, "That moose is not worried about noise. He already thinks we are another moose. We are better off slogging along after him just trying to close the distance." With that said, it was now a full push to get near the quarry.

Finally, after about an hour of trying to cut the moose off, Corey stepped around a lonely spruce tree growing amongst the alders and spotted the moose peeking out from behind a poplar. The hunter made a well-placed shot and put an end to a very frustrating hunt.

If you are using the canoe as a method of travel to still-hunt through heaths and bogs along a waterway, you will do well to follow the advice I offer in the still-hunting section.

Be prepared to exit the canoe frequently in order to see over the banking and scrutinize your surroundings. Because of this, I recommend wearing hip boots or at least good knee-high rubber boots, since the hunter often will find himself out of the canoe as much as in it. Murphy's Law comes into play: "What can go wrong will go wrong and at the worst possible time!" Sometimes the best place to stop for a look around is not going to be the ideal spot to beach a canoe. Be prepared!

Safety while hunting from a canoe is very important. Often there will be other people in the canoe, but the man in the bow is the only person who needs to have a loaded gun. The paddler, and if there is a third person seated in the middle, should keep their guns unloaded until they exit the canoe, since a loaded gun in the back of the canoe is going to point forward at the bowman.

Always keep the gun that is loaded pointed in the air and never at the bottom of the canoe. Accidentally shooting a hole in the canoe is not something you want to happen. The water is cold during moose-hunting season, and the occupants of the canoe will be wearing heavy clothes and boots that can fill with water and pull a man under in seconds. Get a good comfortable lifejacket and wear it! Inflatable suspender life vests are ideal for hunting from a canoe. They give you freedom of movement will not interfere with shooting. Even while hopping in and out of the canoe all day, you will soon forget that you have it on. To me, it is one of the best investments you can make before beginning a canoe hunt.

Always make sure that you know your canoe ahead of time. Know what the load limits are and do not try to surpass them. A canoe loaded to the gunwales going across a flat lake is one thing; add a chop to the water and you have a recipe for swamping.

Also, know what your canoe is going to do should you shoot from it. Occasionally you may be forced to hunt from a small fourteen- to sixteen-foot canoe to get back into some small waterways or bogs. If this is the case, a hunter needs to realize that shooting at a right angle to the canoe may cause it to tip precariously with the recoil of the rifle. I learned this the hard way while duck hunting when I was younger. Believe me, everyone in the canoe is rather shocked to find himself or herself underwater after the gun is fired.

Again, remember Murphy's Law: Anytime water is involved, especially cold water, be prepared for things to really go wrong!

A moose that is standing on the bank of a stream when it is shot, if given a chance, will invariably turn and run back into the water to die. When shooting from a canoe, it is very important to pay close attention to shot placement. Anyone planning a canoe hunt would do well to practice shooting as if they were in a canoe. Practice shooting forward, left, and right from a seated position.

The person who is going to be handling the canoe should spend some time before the hunt getting to know the craft and learning what will make it turn right and left, if it is not something he does every day. He or she has to figure out what to do to stop the canoe in moving water with a pick pole, and hold it steady so that the shooter can make the best shot possible.

This pop-up blind is all set up for an evening hunt. Additional branches have been placed around the blind to break up its outline.

STAND HUNTING

Hunting from a fixed stand, whether it is a ground blind or a tree stand, is not normally my first preference for hunting moose. It does, however, have its place as a hunting technique and should be considered when the opportunity presents itself for a trophy moose.

The key to successful stand hunting is obviously setting up in an area that moose frequent. If a hunter prefers to hunt from a stand, he should look for feeding areas first. No matter what the rut activity, at least the cow moose are going to be feeding, and the cows will draw the bulls. If your hunt falls during the post-rut period, the bulls are going to be putting the feed bag on as well. Clear-cuts and heaths on the water are good first choices because they provide the foods that a moose is looking for, and offer a good field of vision.

Although a good field of vision is important, it is not as important as setting your stand where the moose are going to be traveling, so that the hunter may get a shot at an effective range of the weapon he chooses. I have seen ideal areas to stand hunt when the field of vision was the first consideration. However, getting a moose to come close enough would have been another proposition. So choose your stand site carefully.

Pre-season observation will tell you a lot about where to set your stand. Even if you only have a day or two to watch an area before your hunt begins, it behooves the stand-bound hunter to make sure he is present at prime feeding times to observe where the moose are coming out and feeding.

As is most often the case of heaths or clear-cuts, trees for tree stands are going to be hard to come by. If you can find one that's suitable, by all means set yourself up in it. However, when no trees are present, you will have to resort to a blind of some sort.

In the heaths that I have experience with, moose travel the shortest distance out in the open between point A and point B. They want to stay in whatever cover they can find for as long as possible. Often a hunter can locate a suitable clump of alders or fir trees to set up in. Once there, build a small ground build to further conceal yourself and your movements, and you should do well.

The new pop-up blinds really shine as a moose-hunting tool. Some of them are large enough to conceal three members of a party comfortably. If you take the time and seal the seams of a pop-up blind, it will keep you dry should it rain. During cold weather, I have even used a small propane heater in these mobile blinds and

This cow moose is at a natural mineral/salt lick. Roadside run-off creates these areas from salt placed on the roads during the winter.

Slush bags can be placed high up in trees to attract moose. A moose wound up pulling this bag down from the tree.

stayed warm all day. Sitting out in the open on a cold, drizzly day is no picnic, but wet, chilly days offer some of the best opportunities for moose hunting, so it is to a hunter's advantage to be well prepared.

Whether using a pop-up or a ground blind you build yourself, make sure you set up with a background that breaks up the structure's outline. You don't want to be standing out as a silhouette that is not natural to your quarry. Also, make sure your blind blends in with regard to color and material. You do not want to be setting a green blind against a brown background. Place a few branches or small trees in front of and behind a pop-up blind to break up its outline, and use only materials that are present in an area to insure that any blind you may build onsite will blend in.

BAIT HUNTING

Maine and many other states and provinces that hold a moose season allow baiting. Placing bait for moose can help attract and hold them in a certain area where the hunter can better his chances.

Actually calling this hunting method "baiting" may be a bit of a stretch. Moose normally eat an average of forty pounds of browse a day, and it is doubtful that the average hunter or guide is going to have the time, energy, and money required to actually carry enough bait to feed several moose. Given that, what the hunter is actually doing when baiting is putting out minerals and salts that the moose find attractive.

Moose have a taste for salt, as evidenced each spring when the roadsides start to clear of snow. As the snow melts and runoff pools in ditches, moose can be found drinking the salty water, and as the vegetation starts to regenerate, the grasses and plant shoots leach the salt into their root systems and into the new green growth. Moose that happen to live near roads that are salted during the winter will feed heavily on the seasoned greens.

There are many commercially manufactured baiting products that contain salt, and these can be purchased from sporting goods dealers. If you do not have access to a dealer for these products, you can simply go to any farm-supply store and buy salt blocks or licks to place in your hunting area. If you use these items, be sure to anchor them securely or place them up high, so that bear will have a hard time getting at them.

Old timers have told me that they used to take burlap bags and fill them with canning salt, then hang the bags from tree limbs. Rain would wash through the bag carrying salt to the ground below, where moose and deer would lick it up. Having used "Slush" made by Buck Expert, a salt and mineral product that comes in a burlap bag, I can tell you that the moose will literally eat the dirt beneath a hanging bag.

Pickling or canning salt is non-iodized and is not as refined as table salt. The granules are bigger, and they clump and form large blocks when they get wet. An eighty-pound bag can be purchased from suppliers for around eight to twelve dollars, and at that price, a hunter can afford to place a lot of salt out in an area. There is a drawback to this technique, however. Other hunters could find the salt and move into the area.

I learned a neat trick from a Canadian moose hunter on concealing the salt. He would find a large puddle or ditch of standing water and pour several bags of pickling salt into it. The larger the puddle, the more salt he would pour in. For example, a puddle that measured ten feet by five feet and approximately one to two feet deep would get treated with seven to ten eighty-pound bags of salt. Once the moose find such a spot, they will often keep returning to it.

Another baiting product that works well is the so-called "moose candy," which often comes in two parts and requires mixing at the bait site. It will bubble up and form a crust that adheres to the logs or rocks that you use as a mixing platform and creates a candy lick of sorts. Usually these products for moose will have a maple flavor and scent to them because maple is one of the moose's favorite foods.

When using a "candy" bait, do not be surprised if you only observe cows and calves responding to it as the rut gets near. When the rut is in full swing, a bull's attention is not on feeding but on breeding. Do not despair if you are only seeing cow and calf activity at your bait sites; the bulls will come around to check on the cows.

If you decide to place bait in your hunting area, do so well in advance of the season; thirty days or more is not too far ahead. To get the moose to find the bait quicker, I often use a moose lure or urine to help draw their attention, and reapply the scents or urine each time I check the site. Once I see evidence of moose using the area, I do away with the additional scent, as the moose are going to be leaving a lot of their own urine and scent at this point.

I often use baiting, as do the guides I work with. We do it in areas we are familiar with and hunt from year to year because either they consistently hold moose or they are breeding areas. The bait sites give us a good place to begin our search in a more defined section of a larger tract of moose habitat. ■

3
CALLING MOOSE

Calling moose is not only the most exciting form of hunting there is, but also one of the most effective . . . and the most complex. More variables come into play in calling than in any other hunting method.

Both sexes of moose are extremely vocal—not just during the rut, but also all year long. A bull moose also uses more than just sounds he can make with his larynx. Bulls communicate by raking trees with their antlers and displaying their racks to one another in a menacing manner.

Often, you not only have to try to appeal to a moose's sense of hearing, but his sense of smell. Depending how close you need to get, you may have to appeal to his sense of sight, as well, with the use of a decoy.

All the moose's senses can protect him, or they can help you call him in. In this chapter, I will discuss the individual uses of each type of call—explaining how it appeals to the moose's senses—and offer suggestions for combinations of various techniques that will lead to a successful and exciting hunt.

Many hunters and guides feel that after a certain date, moose will not respond to a call. In Maine, that means after our September hunt, calling is over. I have heard this opinion expressed by guides I consider good woodsmen, for the most part. They just refuse to believe moose can be called in any later in the season.

This is such an old wives tale that I have to wonder what else these guides do not see. Maryo and I, and other guides I work with, consistently call in moose each year during the second hunt in October.

Moose respond differently during the off-peak times of the rut, but they still respond to a call. Not all the cows come into heat the exact same week. Those that are not all bred will come in again. Bulls know this.

Through the use of moose urine, you can trigger a bull into thinking there is a cow in heat in the area you are hunting, causing him to go full bore back into rutting mode.

Maryo has observed his captive moose mating as late as January, and he saw a fetus approximately six months along in development in a cow that was killed on a hunt in Newfoundland during the second week of September. She came into heat at an odd time, but she found a bull that wanted to breed. If that bull was willing to breed, he was willing to respond to her calls.

The bark from this birch tree was cut away and used to make a birch bark moose call.

TYPES OF CALLS

Moose calls can be broken down to three categories: those that use your own voice, electronic calls, and mechanical calls that you pull or blow into.

Using your own voice as a call has worked for centuries. I am sure it goes back to the very first Native Americans who relied on moose as sustenance. While a human with a little practice can do a good job of imitating a bull grunt or a cow in heat, you will still need an amplifier of some sort to help duplicate that deep sound the bull makes, as well as to project the cow-in-heat call farther than you can with your voice unaided.

On the days when sound carries well, I've watched guides use just their voices and cupped hands to project moose sounds. But most of the good voice callers I have been around will carry some sort of megaphone—and I have seen just about every kind of megaphone.

George Perry, a guide from Lincoln, Maine, uses a traditional birch bark call, which is nothing more than a funnel made of birch bark. Such calls are still used by many Quebec moose hunters, and they are one of the most sought-after items that every moose hunter wants to own. I have used George's birch bark call, and I have to tell you it sounds excellent in both tone and volume enhancement. I have also made them myself, and always ended up giving them away to clients who saw me use them.

There is not much to making one of these. Simply find a large white birch tree at least fourteen or more inches in diameter. Cut the bark all the way around the

Butch Phillips of the Penobscot Nation shows one of his birch bark moose calls. His birch bark calls are some of the most rugged calls on the market today. Note how the ends are reinforced with stitching.

circumference of the tree, being careful to make the cut deep enough so that you strike the wood. Measure down about fifteen to eighteen inches and make another cut, parallel to the first one. Now connect the two cuts with a vertical cut and carefully peel the bark from the tree in a solid sheet.

Roll the bark into a cone shape. Traditionally the ending seam is stitched with a rawhide lace or grass. George's call is held together with black electrical tape, and I have done this as well. It takes a lot less time than hand lacing, and it is just as effective.

Butch Phillips, of the Penobscot Indian Nation in Maine, handcrafts what has to be the prettiest birch bark moose call ever made. He learned his craft from tribal elders, as this is a heritage that is passed on from generation to generation. I have had the opportunity to try one of Butch's calls and I've met other hunters who rely on them. He takes great care in choosing the proper tree and removes the bark carefully to get the desired thickness, so he can make a call that will last. Butch told me that over his life, he has taken twenty some-odd moose with his calls.

I saw another unique megaphone that was crafted by Ron Pickard of Frenchville, Maine—a cone of fiberglass with walls thick enough to let him use it as a rattling antler. I've also seen calls made from black tar paper and from the roll-up plastic sled many of us had as kids. One caller I worked with even used a cheerleader megaphone. It was kind of large to carry around, but it sounded very good.

Commercial manufacturers of calls, such as Buck Expert, make a cone for use by voice callers. But any cone-shaped item will work as a megaphone to a degree. Just make sure that whatever you choose does not have a "tinny" tone. It should

To make your own tin can moose call, use a No. 10 can (often used in commercial food establishments) and knot a leather lace or flat shoelace from the inside.

produce the bull grunt, deep and flat, and also be able to project the cow-in-heat call with a medium-high pitch, and without any hollow sound.

Electronic calls, made by a couple of different manufacturers, will produce the cow-in-heat call, various bull sounds, calf sounds, tree-raking, a cow moose urinating, along with some other sounds that can be useful when calling moose.

Here in Maine, we are not allowed to use electronic calls at the present time. I am not a fan of these anyway. For the stationary hunter, I think they have their advantages, but the hunter on the move, or speed calling, is going to find them time consuming to set up and take down. With speed calling, you move from one area to the next very fast, often only spending ten to fifteen minutes at each high-percentage spot. With an electronic call, you may be limited to one tone and pitch for the cow in heat. Many times, you'll need to carry a couple of mouth-operated calls by the same manufacturer, as they will all sound just slightly different in tone and pitch. This will allow you to work a bull more than once if you muff him the first time you try calling him.

Another thing I do not like about the electronic calls are their speakers. In some conditions they sound great, other times they seem

When the wet string is pulled and stretched, the sound resonates out from the inside of the can, simulating either a cow-in-heat call or a bull grunt (depending on the length of the pull).

very tinny. Weather conditions are going to vary greatly day to day. Moisture in the air or no moisture, the temperature is going to effect how a call sounds and the distance that the sound carries. Surrounding trees and vegetation, and any echo effect of the landscape and terrain, are factors that to determine the sound you get. When you consider all of these variables, you can see how they can affect a speaker's performance.

Mechanical calls vary in type as well. Hunters use everything from the coffee can to commercially made mouth calls.

The coffee can call is popular with novice moose hunters. With little or no effort, you can produce a cow-in-heat call or a bull grunt. With little-to-no cost, you can have a few different cans to produce varying pitches and tones. A person can easily learn which can to take out, depending on its sound quality for the given conditions.

To make a call of this kind, you need a coffee can or any other tin can of the same size. Use a nail to punch a hole in the center of the bottom of the can and then thread a leather lace or flat shoelace at least twenty inches long through the hole in the bottom, so it comes out outside the can. Tie a knot on the end inside the can, so the cord you've used cannot be pulled through the hole.

Back when I used a can call, I liked the institutional, or number-eleven, size vegetable can for my calls. I would wrap the outside wall with a layer of carpeting and glue it in place. This would remove the tinny sound. For my laces, I preferred a leather rawhide strip. But, I also had a call with a heavy flat shoelace, just to be able to have two different sounds.

To make the call work, you simply wet the string. Hold the can by the lip under your arm or in your left hand. At the outside end of the can, place the lace between your index finger and thumb, and squeeze the string. Pull it tight and allow your fingers to slide down the string. It may take a few tries to determine the correct pressure you need to apply. The sound is made from the string vibrating due to the pulling pressure you are applying, and the knot vibrating on the can bottom. You pull the string the entire length to get a cow-in-heat call, and make short pulls to get the bull grunt.

It is amazingly simple! With a little practice, most of the time you can be reproducing the two major sounds you need to make. Notice I said most of the time.

The wrong pressure, or a string that is too wet or too dry, and you might make a bad sound. Making a bad sound is a bad thing when trying to call any animal, let alone a moose.

I will admit, when I was using the can call, I found it worked great during the peak of the rut. At the peak of the rut, a moose will respond to the distant sound of a wood harvester saw blade screeching through a log. At times of peak rut, I swear you can call a moose with car horn. But during those days prior to peak and after peak rut, the tin can call is an iffy proposition at best. Plus it requires a lot of movement to work the call. Additionally, it cannot be used in conjunction with a hand-held decoy; a can call is just too cumbersome. Although it can work during the peak rut, it just is not a good all-around call.

Mouth-operated calls are by far the best I have found. Back when I used the can call, I could not find a mouth call that sounded like a moose. Some manufacturers actually took a deer call, added a megaphone to it, and sold it as a moose call. I saw one call that was actually a badly tuned elk call. In those days, I used my voice along with the can call.

The first time I heard a Buck Expert moose call demonstrated, I knew it was going to change the way I called. I could not buy one fast enough. It was a little difficult learning to use the first models Maryo came out with. I compared it to mastering a musical instrument. It took practice, and lots of it. But the first season I used the call, I knew that every bit of time I had put into practicing was worth it.

Since Buck Expert moose calls have been so successful, many companies now are copying the concept of the open-reed system developed by Maryo. A number of manufacturers have changed their products to better match the Buck Expert line of moose calls. As with all other calls, some manufacturers have been able to duplicate the proper sounds, while others leave a lot to be desired. You will have to try out various calls and compare them to see what I mean.

Since the introduction of Buck Expert's first moose call, Maryo has strived to make a call that is more user friendly. In 2005, he came out with his X-Treme Moose Call, which has made long practice periods a thing of the past. In field tests conducted during the 2004 Maine moose-hunting season, guides who had never had a chance to practice on this call were calling in moose on their first try with it.

Not a company to leave well enough alone, Buck Expert will be introducing easier calls for the beginner to use in the future.

HOW MOOSE COMMUNICATE

There is just no way, through the written word, that I can accurately describe the sounds a moose makes, which is why I decided to make a CD of moose sounds, including an explanation of each one. No matter what type of call you may decide to use, you can learn to duplicate the sounds provided on the CD.

These are the types of sounds you should learn, and explanations of the differences between them:

COW-IN-HEAT CALL: The sound of a cow in heat is one of the top-two communications a moose hunter should know how to reproduce; a good hunter will find himself using it more than any other. It is also one of the most misinterpreted sounds. Many a moose caller has failed to reproduce it correctly and unintentionally pushed moose away or caused them to hang up.

The sound the cow in heat makes differs from that produced by a cow that's not in heat. It will also vary depending on the stage of her heat. A cow-in-heat call sounds off high and the tone actually quivers. It will rise near the end and then fade off softly, varying in duration from three seconds to as much as fifteen seconds, depending on her degree of agitation.

The key to a good cow-in-heat call is the quiver in the tone and soft fade out. Many moose callers, when they are just learning this type of call, tend to make the mistake of chopping the sound off abruptly. You may hear this sound in the wild made by an actual cow moose. When a cow ends her call abruptly, she is saying to the bull, "I am in heat but I have a headache right now. Tag along if you want." A bull will come close, then just hang back, waiting for her to call that she is ready to accept him. This is one reason why beginning moose callers have so many bulls hang on them. They are just saying the wrong words in moose language.

A moose will also vary its volume so a caller can too. As you start off calling, you may want to project the call loudly. It is advisable to use a megaphone to increase the volume. As a bull comes closer to your position, tone your calls down, decrease your volume, and discontinue using the megaphone.

A cow moose is in heat for a twenty-four-hour period. During this time she

Gary Wadsworth, me, and his son Curt on their first Maine moose hunt. This was the first moose I called in with the Buck Expert moose call.

will call constantly to find a bull. At the Buck Expert Research Center in Quebec, they have found that a cow in heat will call up to six hundred times in a twenty-four-hour period. I know, I have listened to a cow calling in the wild for an hour or more and lost track of the number of times she sounded off. I do not think you can over call in most cases to get a bull started.

BULL GRUNTS: The bull makes two very distinct grunts. One grunt says to the cow, "I'm in love." The other says, to other bulls, "I want to fight." A caller should learn both. At a distance, the two calls are going to sound the same, but once the bull moose gets within one hundred yards of the caller, the sound will be noticeably different.

The Buck Expert moose call is the only one I have found to date that can successfully duplicate the bull grunt as well as the cow calls. I use it to grunt when a bull is a long distance out from me; the megaphone really increases the volume and sounds much deeper than I can make the sound with my voice.

Once the bull gets within one hundred yards or closer, depending on how the sound is carrying, I may switch over to my voice. The Buck Expert call reproduces the "I'm-in-love" grunt perfectly—just a simple "Orrrhh."

As he gets closer to the cow, the moose will typically lower his volume. If I want to sound like another bull that is with a cow or approaching a cow, I need to tone my volume down as well. I also do not want to sound bigger than the moose I'm calling. A moose will try to intimidate rivals with his grunts. As a rule of thumb, the deeper a grunt, the larger the bull.

If the moose is coming in and wants to fight, I will switch over to do my bull grunts using my voice and a megaphone. There will be an audible "click" before the "I-want-to-fight" grunt. You can duplicate this sound two ways. The first way is to smack your lips as if you were chewing a big wad of gum. Smack your lips loudly. It will sound even more convincing if you have a substantial amount of saliva in your mouth when you do this. The sound should come off as "Smack Orrrhh."

The second method is the one I use: Place your tongue on the roof of your mouth and suck back while pulling your tongue from the roof of your mouth. It will make a very loud sound that should come off as "Click Orrrhh."

Depending on how big and how mad you might want to sound to another moose, you can draw out the sound of your grunt by exhaling more into the megaphone and extending the "hhhh." It should sound like "Orrrhhhhh . . . ." Taper it down slowly. The madder the bull gets, the meaner he wants to sound. You want to convince the other moose that you are trying to provoke him. So the madder he sounds, make sure you sound just as mad.

ANTLER SOUNDS: Bull moose use their antlers to communicate with other moose. The bull will not only use his antlers to provoke rivals—the larger the rack, the more sound it makes—but also to answer cow calls.

It is believed that when a bull moose rakes his antlers in response to a cow call, he is trying to impress the female by showing that he is the dominant bull in the area. His display is telling her, "Hey babe! I am the biggest guy here. Listen to this."

I have had more than one bull respond to a cow call with nothing more than raking. I also believe it may be a sign of sexual frustration. I think they do this, at times, because they can hear and smell the cow, but cannot see her. These actions are often seen when bull moose get close to the caller.

Master Maine guide Hal Blood called in a bull for some clients on a hunt. The bull immediately responded to the cow calls he made and moved right to where Hal and the hunters were waiting, thinking it was where the cow should be. When he did not see a cow, the bull walked up to an alder clump and proceeded to start shredding it. While he was occupied venting his frustration, a hunter was able to shoot it at a distance of less than twenty yards. This bull had clearly been antagonized by the fact that he heard a cow, came looking for her, and could not find her, so he had attempted to lure her out in the open by using his antlers.

Because bulls use their antlers as a form of communication, other moose know the difference between the sounds of a large set and a small set. A caller wants to keep this in mind when including raking as a part of his calling repertoire. If a caller is raking and sounds too much like a large moose, he may scare away a moose that decides he is smaller than the beast making the opposing sounds. (More on this later.)

MOOSE HUNTING

The most perfect item to duplicate the sound of a moose antler is just that, a moose antler. A hunter who rakes with an actual moose antler is going to sound just like the real thing. I bought and carry a moose shed that weighs five pounds and fits nicely on my hip, where I wear my fanny pack.

A moose with a five-pound antler is going to be in the two- to three-year age bracket on average. Bernard Metivier of Quebec uses an antler lighter than mine because he does not like to sound big at all.

Corey Kinney, on the other hand, used to lug around an antler that weighed in at over ten pounds—equivalent to one on a three- to five-year-old bull, with a larger palm than mine. While Corey was using that huge antler, he never got a small moose to show himself, and I never knew him to kill a bull less than fifty inches. I lugged that antler for him and did the raking on more than one occasion. It took the use of both my hands to make it sound convincing.

The antler I use is approaching ten years old at the time I am writing this. I always make sure that I soak it in a tub of water prior to the hunting season. The soaking adds close to a half-pound to the weight of the antler, but it takes out the hollow tin sound that is common with a dried antler. Maybe I am just too picky in the sounds that I try to reproduce, but my pickiness has yielded me some good-size moose throughout the years.

Some callers have found other ways of imitating the antler sound, and the items they use to help them are as varied as calling techniques. My great-grandfather talked to me about an ash canoe paddle that was his preferred method of raking. I still have his paddle, and I can tell you that when it's held properly in my hand and raked in a poplar tree, it sounds very convincing.

I have known some Canadian callers to use the brow paddle from a caribou

Rick Dodge (aka Fudge) likes to use a moose shoulder blade for raking bushes when calling. It is lighter than an antler and has good tone.

antler as a raking antler. It sounds very hollow, yet not intimidating to other moose as they approach, and is light in weight for easy carrying.

Many callers like to use a dried shoulder blade from a butchered moose as a raking tool. It sounds great, producing good volume and excellent tone, and it can be rubbed on anything from a six-inch popular tree to a stand of alders to get the desired sounds. The drawback to using a shoulder blade is that they do become brittle and break, and once a shoulder blade develops a split, the sound quality greatly diminishes. If you desire to use a shoulder blade bone, let it soak in water before the season begins to keep it from drying out and breaking, and to take away some of the tinny sound that you may get with an over-dried bone.

The award for the weirdest item used has to go to master guide Dan Glidden of Maine, who was working as a guide for Corey and I. His client had shot an exceptionally large moose with a spread of over fifty inches. Since Dan did not have a cameraman with him at the time of the kill, we did some after-the-fact filming. While the hunter was relating the story for the camera, he mentioned a sports-drink bottle that Danny rattled in the bushes. Corey and I looked at each other and shrugged our shoulders and let the hunter and Dan continue with their story.

As we were taking down the camp, Corey and I cornered Dan and said, "What is the thing with the sports-drink bottle?"

Dan smiled and kicked the dirt at his feet and told us this story:

"You guys all carry those big antlers for raking. I hate to lug more than I have to. I found that a plastic liter-size bottle on a hardwood stick rattled in the bushes sounds as good as an antler. Sheds that I find in the winter are worth a lot of money, so why am I going to keep one for me? I can go to the dump and find a plastic sports-drink bottle, whittle a stick to fit in the end, and I am all set."

Dan then demonstrated his "Bottle Antler," and I must say it sounded good. I am a firm believer in it to this day, and carry one in my truck in case I lose my antler, or loan it out to a starting moose guide.

You can make one yourself from any one-liter plastic bottle; I have used sports drink and liquor bottles made of plastic. Cut the bottom end out of the bottle, leaving a three-quarter-inch lip all around so that it retains some rigidity. Next, whittle a hardwood stick to a tapered point to fit inside the bottle spout. This should extend through the neck and into the body of the bottle, but not come out the end that you have cut off.

Force the bottle onto the stick so you won't lose it. Cut the opposite end off the stick to the length you want. (Dan prefers to leave his long; it doubles as walking stick for him.) And there you have your moose antler on a stick!

Some callers like to hunt as light as they can. Ron Pickard made his fiberglass megaphone call heavy enough so that he can use it as a rattling antler. The sound Ron gets from his megaphone is excellent, and it allows him to carry only the one piece of gear. He uses his voice through the megaphone as a call, and has the megaphone to rake on trees if he needs to.

Buck Expert has taken this one step further. Maryo designed a call that has

Nine-year-old DJ McHugh of Monmouth, Maine, called in this fifty-plus inch bull for his dad Dennis. DJ used a birch bark call he and his father made together. The bull was one of the largest taken in Maine in 2005, weighing in at 1,050 pounds.

a megaphone made from a plastic composite, with a serrated edge on it. Due to the plastic's composition, when this megaphone is scraped on trees and bushes, it sounds just like a moose antler. Mario went through a lot of trial and error to get the sound right, and the new call was released in 2005.

The first year we tested the call, it was unbelievable. After demonstrating it in the camp yard, guides were leaving their raking antlers in the trucks each morning—they had that much faith in the sound of the megaphone as a raking antler. This innovation by Buck Expert has lightened the load of the guides that I am associated with.

Making the sounds that a moose makes with his antlers calls for some visualization on the caller's part. He or she needs to remember that the moose is a big, lumbering animal.

A moose does not toss his head back and forth as quickly as a whitetail buck. He moves his head as an animal his size would, in a slow and lumbering manner, but with power and strength. When raking an antler, you have to move it as a moose would to get the correct sound: slowly, deliberately, with some force. If you imagine that you are as big as a moose and trying to move all that headgear around, you will make the required sounds that much more convincing.

A moose wants to make sure that others are hearing him as well. When he twists his head from left to right with his antlers in an alder bush, he hesitates at the end of his rake just for a second before twisting back in the other direction. Make sure, when you rake, that you duplicate this rhythm, moving from left to right or right to left, pausing at the end of each swing for a split second before coming back the other way.

Also, make note of his vocalization pattern. He will not grunt while he is raking, but rather will stop the procedure, lift his head, and then grunt. A moose does not hear another moose grunting while it is raking, so the hunter should not make grunting sounds when raking, either. Do it after and before the raking sequence.

As a caller, the volume you put out during the raking will also determine whether or not you are going to see the moose. Too much antler noise will drive away a smaller bull, and on more than one occasion I have had moose come in and hang up. The animal in question and I would call back and forth, challenging each other. He would refuse to show himself. I would call. He would call. He would rake. I would rake. This pattern led me to believe that he had doubts about himself being dominant. At this point, a caller must decide what to do.

Hunting in Maine, I usually have an abundance of moose to choose from, and this greatly influences my decision to be more aggressive in my calling. At this stage in my moose conversation, I normally try to sound like I am a bigger moose than he is. I will thrash my antler menacingly in a bush and grunt loudly, wanting him to think that I am a rival bull that is mad with rage, so the other moose will challenge me.

One of two things will happen. He will either say, "Hey! I am bigger than you," and step out, or he will grunt back as he retreats into the woods, as if to say, "Okay, you win."

This is a dandy bull I called in during the 2005 hunting season.

CALLING TIPS

If there is one saying that can be applied to moose calling, it is, "Practice makes perfect." Start practicing with your moose call well in advance to the season. If your family does not want you practicing in the house, do it when you are driving in your car alone. You want to be able to blow into the call each time and get a perfect sound from it. Bad notes when calling will hurt you more than not calling at all.

When first learning to call, do not get discouraged on those days when you get no responses from a bull. It happens to the best moose callers. Just figure that you were not near enough to an animal that wanted to come out and play with you.

Pay close attention each time you call in a bull. Even if it is not a trophy moose, learn from it. Understand what you did to bring that moose to you.

When you finally call in a couple of moose, continue to use that style of successful calling as your primary technique. If you consistently return to an area to call, remember to vary your technique. Let the bull that heard your primary sequence think that he is responding to a different cow.

Never start your calling sequence before legal shooting time. A bull could be very close to you and show up too early. On those dark, overcast days when daylight takes forever to finally arrive, do not call until your hunters tell you they can see into the woods well enough to shoot.

If you feel you must call before legal light to locate your moose, use this trick I learned quite by accident a few years ago. Carry an owl call and blow into it imitating the "who, who, who cooks for you" call of the barred owl. I have heard moose respond to this call in the night and early morning hours before daylight. When I first mentioned this to Maryo, he said that many old-time Quebec moose hunters had told him the same thing.

When I use this trick to locate a moose, I plan on only getting one grunt from him immediately at the end of the owl call, so make sure you and others with you are listening closely to be able to pinpoint his location. You will only get one chance if he decides to respond to the owl call.

Never assume that you know exactly where the bull is going to come from. Instead, play the wind so it works in your favor. At times this might require you to take a longer route into an area to come in on the downwind side.

Carry more than one call with you while hunting. You could lose or break one. Additionally, even though the same company might have made your calls, they will sound slightly different in tone and/or pitch. This allows you to work the same bull more than once and keep him from getting suspicious.

If you make a mistake with a bull one day and go back in on him later in the week, call to him from a different location within his area. Do not give him anything that will make him more suspicious than he already is going to be.

When walking and calling, if you return to your starting spot via the same route, stop at all the places you called on your trip in and call again. A bull may have responded and you did not hear him. He may still be in the area looking for the cow he heard. ■

4
DECOYS FOR MOOSE

Decoys for moose work because of the animal's very poor eyesight. Moose are extremely vocal and, for the most part, they like each other's company. During the breeding season, the bulls want to be with cows and cows want to be with bulls. It is at this point that a moose's natural instinct makes him most vulnerable and hunters can use this to their advantage.

I like to think of decoying moose as a supplement to calling them. I have tried to use a decoy alone, and it just does not work. But using a decoy in conjunction with calling will help get a moose inside the range of the weapon you are using.

To understand how a decoy works, one must first have knowledge of how a moose sees. With its limited eyesight, the moose can only see in focus for a distance of ten to fifteen feet. He relies mainly on shape and movement, rather than color.

If you have ever seen a moose walking down a road directly toward you, you

Maryo Pepin prepares a prototype decoy for testing.

would see a rack, head, neck, chest, and legs. You would not see his hind end. This is exactly how the moose sees a properly utilized decoy.

At present, a hunter has three choices for moose decoys. Although one type may be more suited to a particular weapon or landscape than another, each has its purpose and place. The terrain hunted may also play a deciding factor on which decoy to use. Most well-rounded moose guides will carry all three decoys with them and know how to use each type to its best advantage.

The first decoy type is the moose antler you are carrying to do your raking with. To use it as a decoy, hold the antler over your head, resting it on your head. Be sure to hold it on the proper side of your head if it is a right side antler or a left side antler. If you are dressed in a dark camouflage outfit and mimicking the lumbering movements of a moose, you will be amazed at how close you can get to a bull! When playing with moose, both Corey and I have closed the distance to within fifteen feet or less using just an antler. Of course, it helped to have a moose that was slobbering all over himself and wanted to fight. The point is, the antler is simple and will work well as a decoy.

Maryo Pepin developed a moose head on a stick as a decoy and perfected its use. The first decoys we had of this type were made of a hollow foam rubber, and they had removable antlers, which made them convenient to transport, and allowed hunters to use them as cows or bulls. A push broom handle was inserted into the neck of the decoy for ease of use and control of the head.

These decoys were extremely cost prohibitive to manufacture, and that cost had to be passed on to the consumer, so they were a little expensive and never really caught on in the marketplace.

Having a need for several of these decoys, Corey and I decided to make our own with the sort of foam form that taxidermists use when making head mounts of moose. Corey cut off some of the neck and the shoulder area to lighten it up, and put the ear inserts on the head with a foam spray adhesive. The antlers are nothing more than plywood cut outs and attached to the form with angle braces. A broom handle was inserted in to the chin area of the foam form for handling and carrying. When this decoy was used properly, we could literally lead a moose around with it.

Using either the antler or the head-on-a-stick requires proper use, and to get the most out of the decoy, your first consideration should be clothing.

The decoy user needs to be wearing a dark camouflage pattern. If your clothing is too light in color, the moose is going to make you out as an impostor long before the decoy has a chance to do its magic and get you close. I wear a dark camo pattern and have had no trouble getting close to moose.

I also wear a facemask and gloves to cover any white skin that is apt to show. I have tried not wearing the mask and gloves and have been busted. But, I have never been busted when I took the time to cover all of my skin. Human skin shows up to a moose.

During our moose season in Maine, we do not have to wear hunter orange unless carrying a firearm. I never wear orange when decoying. It shows up to a moose like a beacon.

When moving with the decoy, the user needs to move like a moose, with a lumbering gait. As a bull becomes agitated, he will stiffen his knees and walk with a rocking motion. He will also be tipping his head from side to side to display his antlers to his adversary. Keep this in mind when using a decoy to close the distance.

If you were to simply hold the decoy and try to walk toward a moose as you walk down a street, that moose will off before you get any closer. I do not care how much he is slobbering on himself. Having experimented with this, I am telling you first hand.

The other key to the antler or the head-on-a-stick decoys is the point of positioning to the moose. Never allow the moose to get in a position where he will be able to see your side profile. If he starts to circle, the decoy holder must move accordingly to allow the moose to only see the head-on view of the decoy and the holder. The decoyer must appear to be another moose at all times for this to work.

The third type of decoy is the silhouette. I helped test the silhouette decoy made by Renzo's Decoys of Wisconsin, and discovered that it has a place in the moose hunter's bag of tricks.

The Renzo's decoy is made of a waterproof coraplast material, and considering that when opened it represents a full-size moose, it folds up relatively small. The decoy comes with a set of antlers that you can add to make it look like a bull, and

Corey and I show the decoys we use and helped to develop. Note the size of Corey's rattling antler.

without the antlers, it can be used as a cow. I have used it both ways. As a cow decoy it really shines in large open areas, such as in clear-cuts or cranberry bogs.

While I refer to this decoy as a silhouette, the decoy is actually a 3-D photographic image of a moose that is quartering. This allows the design to be a little bit smaller than a full-size side profile of a moose. When you have to carry the decoy for a stalking situation, the quartering view allows you to make a natural approach due to what the moose is seeing. The 3-D photographic image is very realistic. So realistic in fact it has been used by game wardens to catch poachers!

It is a good decoy to use in situations where a hunter or caller might have to wear hunter orange to be in accordance with the law. The decoy holder and hunter can get behind the decoy and use one of the fold-down viewing flaps to see out, which allows the users to stay hidden from the moose's view at all times. This decoy is no different than the other two I have already covered in that it needs to be used properly if it's going to work.

When first testing the Renzo's decoy near a remote pond in the north Maine woods region one Sunday afternoon, Corey and I got a chance to see just how bad a moose's eyesight is, which helped us learn the proper way to put the device to use.

We arrived at the shore of the pond, which was bordered by a floating heath. The plan was for Corey to be the cameraman and for me to be with the decoy. A wrong step in the heath meant that we would be up to our hips in mud and water. The heath had many uprooted trees that, from a distance, had the shape and appearance of moose turned at various angles.

Once we made sure that none of the uprooted trees were moose, I made a cow-in-heat call. Instantly we had a response from a bull. Corey had guided a hunter through the area the week before and come in contact with many moose that his client had decided not to shoot. We knew full well that we would be dealing with educated moose.

A bull showed on the far side of the pond and started toward us. We both knew that he could not see the decoy and was more intent on following the cow-in-heat calls I was making.

The bull had to swim across an inlet of the pond in order to reach us. Once he reappeared in our view, at a distance of about three hundred yards, he grunted a couple of times. I cow called back at him, and he proceeded to start to walk away. Stunned, I looked back at Corey as if to say, "Now what did I do?" Corey made a motion for me to move the decoy.

With another cow call, I got the bull to stop and look in my direction. While he was looking my way, I moved the decoy, mimicking the movements of a moose walking across the heath. Instantly he focused on the decoy and began to come toward me. Due to the uprooted trees and other stunted spruces, he lost sight of me from time to time. He would stop and grunt, and I made sure to move the decoy so he could see it, which would get an immediate positive response from the bull as he continued toward me.

Without having to move myself more than fifty feet, I got this particular bull to come within twenty yards of me. He finally winded me and that was the end of the game, but Corey had been able to capture the entire episode on film. We not only were pleased with how the Renzo's decoy worked, but also gained a lot of insight into moose behavior.

First, as stated before, we were dealing with moose that had recently been called to. He came to a certain point and was going to move away. With all the uprooted trees on that heath, I am sure he saw a lot of dark shapes that could have been moose. But since none of them moved, he felt uncertain of his judgment and decided to get out of there. Once I started to move the decoy so he could see it, he was sure I was the cow in question and he closed the distance. Fairly quickly, I might add.

Even though I was using cow-in-heat urine to cover my scent, I am sure that bull could still smell me. I distinctly remember not being very careful with my clothing that day, since we were only testing a decoy rather than hunting. That is why he chose to try and circle me. Once he got into a good wind cone and caught my scent, he knew he had been duped and got out of there in a hurry.

CHOOSING THE PROPER DECOY

Once you have a good understanding of the types of decoys, you must decide which one, if any, is right for a particular hunt. There are certain factors that I take into consideration when choosing a decoy for a particular hunt. The first factor is the weapon that the hunter is using.

For the center-fire-rifle hunter, I am content to either carry just an antler or nothing at all. I will not bother with a decoy if I know that the terrain or landscape features are not going to allow an animal to spot the decoy before it is too late for the moose's well-being.

If I am going to be walking a winter road or working around a clear-cut that offers long-range visibility, the antler alone will be enough to get me and the hunter within a 150-yard range almost every time.

The muzzleloader or handgun hunter requires me to get him inside the one hundred-yard mark. I realize that today's modern muzzleloaders and handguns make shots out to longer ranges possible. Based on my years of experience, I like to get as close as I can.

If I know that I am going to be able to see out to three hundred yards or more, and want to close that distance by two thirds, or more, I will more than likely carry the head-on-a-stick decoy. For the most part, the antler may work, but I want to make sure the moose will go for the decoy. The head on stick can be more convincing when it comes to provoking a moose, giving him more to focus on. He will become more agitated with the decoy holder because he sees both antlers of the decoy sway from side to side in an intimidating way.

For the bow hunter, terrain plays into the equation more than any other time. If I am in an area that is big and open, such as a heath or cranberry bog, given the option, I will go with the silhouette decoy. It allows me to not only conceal both the shooter and myself from the moose's view, but also to make more movement with a bigger object in order to catch the animal's attention.

If I am going to be hunting a winter road or trail situation with a bow hunter, I may decide to take the head on a stick. It lets me get the moose to the road, keep him in front of me, and still be able to close the distance for a decent bow-shot.

If I were bow hunting in an area that doesn't offer me much more than a fifty-yard field of view, I would take an antler only—trying to make sure that I have an extra caller along with me to help out. The extra caller, or guide, would stay with the hunter to judge the animal and watch the shot placement. If I lack another caller to help out and still opt to use the antler as a decoy, I want to make sure that I trust the hunter in his abilities to judge a trophy animal, and to follow up on the animal's reactions once the arrow is released.

In having discussed the various techniques for using a decoy, I have given the scenarios that best suit specific decoy types. But these are best-case scenarios and guidelines; in no way do the techniques I mention rule out other possible combinations. I have had to use the silhouette-type decoy with rifle hunters who were incapable of making a two hundred-yard shot. Knowing full well that I had to get a moose inside fifty to seventy-five yards to make a clean kill prompted my decision. Remember, use your judgment and let the hunter's ability and terrain make the call when deciding which decoy to carry.

USING THE DECOY

I have already said that when using an antler or head-on-a-stick decoy, hunters should wear dark clothing and cover all exposed skin, such as the hands and face.

You need to move like a moose in a lumbering fashion. This is easy with only one man behind the decoy. But if you are using the decoy, you are probably not the shooter. You just do not have enough hands to be able to call, hold onto the decoy, and a weapon. So there is going to be another hunter behind you while you do your best to close the distance—and this is where pre-hunt instructions are very important.

As the decoy handler, you will need to have total faith in the hunter behind you. This person is going to have a loaded weapon of one sort or another. And do not forget the adrenaline factor that goes along with being so close to such a large animal.

When using the antler or head on a stick, the decoy handler and hunter are going to walk in tandem, decoy handler in front and hunter behind. As the moose may move to the side, the decoy handler is going to step so that the moose can only see a head-on view of the decoy. The hunter has to be very in tune with what the handler is doing. He needs to move in unison with the decoy handler, step for step, motion for motion, and to be so close that if the handler stops quickly, the hunter will run into him.

The hunter also has to rely on the decoy handler to make the judgment call when the moose is close enough—to be able to read the moose's reactions. If the moose is within range and the handler decides that he is not going to get any closer or get a better shot, the shooter needs to be able to react quickly.

The handler may be able to communicate with the shooter in low whispers . . . and I do mean LOW! You may very well be in a situation where you are close enough to hear the moose breathe. If you can hear him, he can hear you, too.

The hunter does not want to be poking his head out around the handler to see the events unfolding. It will look very unnatural to the moose. Every time I have been busted using a decoy, it was because the hunter decided to peek out around me to watch what was happening. That has spooked every moose I have encountered with the decoy and a hunter, so I cannot emphasize enough that the hunter needs to have all the faith in the world in the decoy handler, and be ready for the moment to shoot.

Is it a moose or a decoy? This is the view a moose would have of the head on a stick decoy.

So when do you shoot? The handler has moved the hunter to well within range for the weapon being used. The animal turns and presents a perfect shot. The decoy handler decides that is when the shot should be taken. He simply steps aside, right or left, while saying in a very low whisper, "Now!"

As a matter of safety, I always move to my right. Always! If I have a bow hunter who is right handed, he is carrying his bow with a nocked arrow, the bow will be in his left hand with the broadhead pointed left and to the ground. His right hand will be on the release and connected to the bowstring. His right elbow should be in my back when I stop short, or I should feel the top limb of his bow in my butt.

If perchance I have a left-handed bow shooter, I whisper, "Now!" and take one step right and one step forward. This gets me out of the way of the hunter bringing the bow into position to shoot.

With gun hunters it is very similar, except that after I step right, I take at least one step back as well, in order to get me away from the muzzle blast of the weapon. I want the right-handed shooter to keep the muzzle down and to the left. I want the left-handed shooter to keep the muzzle pointed up at the sky, bringing the weapon down to the aim point when ready.

The reason I always step to the right is that it eliminates the guesswork on the part of my hunter. He knows full well which direction I will move and can plan on it when I say, "Now!" You may find it is easier to move left, and by all means, work around that accordingly. But be sure to tell your hunter which way you are going to move!

I also tell my hunters that I do not want to feel the broadhead in my leg, and I do not want to hear that all-too-familiar "snick" of a safety going off until I say the word. If I feel or hear either one before we are in range, I'll give the word, game over!

Let me run through a couple of scenarios that have happened to me.

SCENARIO 1: I have a gun hunter. He can only shoot comfortably about seventy-five yards on a range, and I feel that once the adrenaline gets going, the distance will be less than that. We are going to hunt a winter road early in the morning, with the wind in our faces. I take only my raking antler from the truck.

After walking and calling a distance, we get a response from a bull. Because I know the road swings in the direction that we hear him, we move down the road to intercept him. Upon arriving at the spot where I think he should be, he appears walking up over a banking. He is only thirty yards from us, but I am in the way of a clean shot.

This has all happened so fast that the hunter does not have time to think. I know he is standing behind me with a loaded rifle. He has previously been instructed as to what to do in this situation.

We move in perfect unison toward the bull. I sway left, so does the hunter. I sway right, he follows perfectly. I close the distance to about twenty feet. The moose starts to circle me to my left, presenting a broadside shot. I step aside right and back one step while whispering, "Now!" The hunter smoothly brings the gun up and wallops him right in the neck, dropping the animal instantly.

It is a perfect example of how a plan can come together. The hunter told me later that he never knew what was happening. He knew I would say when, and which direction I would move to get out of the way. When he saw the moose so close, he said that he kind of froze for a second. From my perspective, you would not have known it; the shot came at the time I figured it should come. The hunter did a commendable job, and not once did I feel I was in danger from him.

SCENARIO 2: It was an afternoon hunt and I had a right-handed bow hunter. We were going to be walking a dead-end logging road. Earlier in the day, I tied a thread across the road so I could see if anyone had driven in ahead of me. When I returned, the thread was intact, indicating that no one had gone by. I took the head-on-a-stick decoy with me when leaving the truck.

The wind was in our faces as we made our way down the road. The plan was to work to the end of the road by dark and come back to the truck with our flashlights. Just before end of legal hunting, I got a response from a bull. We waited to see how he was going to approach us. When his line of travel was determined, we backed up the road to allow him to come out in the open.

The small bull stepped into the road. He looked confused, as he had heard a cow in heat before and now here was this bull, my decoy, challenging him to duel. He accepted the challenge and started moving toward us.

The hunter had been pre-informed as to what was going to happen, and where I was going to step, and when I thought I would call the shot. I also told him that I would call the yardage as we moved closer. I knew his maximum range to be thirty yards, and planned on getting him much closer than that.

We closed the distance to twenty yards. The hunter did a perfect job of matching me step for step and turn for turn with the bull. Once I felt the upper limb of the bow touch my butt. A lot better than the broadhead!

At twenty yards, the bull started to cut to the left, presenting a good quartering shot. I stepped sideways while saying the word to shoot. The hunter raised the bow, drew and released.

I would like to tell you that all went well from that point on. Not a chance! He "jumped the string" trying to watch the arrow find its mark. Unfortunately, by doing that, he lowered the bow at the moment of release, the arrow found dirt under the belly of the moose, and away he went.

It was a perfect stalk on both our parts. We both did everything "by the book," right up to the moment of the release. He admitted to me that he'd "jumped the string," and that he could not have asked for a better opportunity. To quote him, "Twenty yards from a quartering forward moose only is exceeded by a twenty-yard quartering-away moose."

While I was quite upset over the ordeal, it was not that big a moose. The hunter got a much bigger bull the next morning, so all worked out well for us.

SAFETY WHEN USING A DECOY

Before the reader gets a moose decoy and heads out into the woods to learn how to use it, there are some safety concerns that one needs to be aware of.

First and foremost are other hunters. Never use a decoy in an area where you may encounter other moose-hunting parties. I prefer to use them in remote locations, such as on dead-end roads, where I can be sure no one is ahead of me. Remote ponds and clear-cuts that are well off the traveled road are other places where I will consider using a decoy. Even in these situations, never assume that you are alone in the area. Keep an eye out and be prepared for other hunters.

When I get out of my vehicle and know I am going to be decoying, I place a sign on the bumper of my truck that reads, "Caution. Moose Decoy In Use." I make the sign big enough and bright enough that it stands out. Three-feet by three-feet square is not too small!

Also, when using a decoy I make sure to have a hunter orange bandanna in an easy-to-reach pocket I can get at in a hurry to wave around if I should spot another hunting party. I have never had to use it to date. But if I had to, I would

This is the sign I leave on the back of my truck when I am hunting with a client and using a decoy. It is important to make sure the sign is a large one!

drop the decoy, pull out the bandanna, and start hollering at the party to let them know that I was not a moose. Do not take anything for granted. Be ready!

The second safety consideration to keep in mind is the unpredictable nature of a wild animal, particularly a moose that you have just agitated. Moose are, for the most part, very docile and wary of humans. Provoke a bull in rut, and you have an animal that is totally blind to anything other than defending his property rights.

Before attempting to use a decoy, I would recommend that you spend considerable time with someone who has been trained in moose behavior. I spent two years with Corey and other callers observing, not only the moose, but also the caller as well, before I even attempted to decoy a moose.

Maryo, Corey, and I have all had moose at ten feet or less from us. The urge is very strong to try and touch the moose, and we all would like to try it—although, after reading the moose at that distance, we all backed off.

On the other hand, I have seen Bernard call "game over" with a moose when it was still at the thirty-foot mark or more, and only once saw him allow a moose to get nose-to-nose with a decoy. As a note, he was not the one holding the decoy! He told Corey and me that some day we will be sorry for playing this game. I am not sure, but I think Bernard has been charged before and it gave him special respect for the animal—more so than someone who has not been in that situation.

I have seen some TV shows done by naturalists who were studying moose and figured out, either from their own or Maryo's research, that moose can be decoyed. I actually saw one program where the guy had the head foam form of a moose strapped to his chest! If I am going to be using a decoy, I want to be able to throw it away in a hurry! Do not even think of doing something this stupid, because you are only asking for trouble. Either death or a major hospital stay awaits.

Take nothing for granted when using a decoy. Another hunter or an agitated moose are your worst nightmares. Use extreme caution, and do not try it unless you have been properly instructed. ■

5
THE USE OF SCENTS

The use of scents alone will bring moose in all by themselves, but you need to remember that for scents to work, a moose must be able to smell them. I prefer to think of scents as another tool in my toolbox ready to be pulled out when calling moose.

There are some good moose scents on the market, just as there are good deer scents. Also, like the deer market, there are a lot of "snake oils" out there as well, and the hunter needs to beware.

Do some research on a company before buying a scent product that claims to be made from moose urine or musk. I only know of one captive moose herd in North America, and it is owned by Quebec's Buck Expert company. Other lure manufacturers may follow their lead in the future, if they get government permits; for now, take the time to find out if the manufacturer of the scent you are planning to buy has access to live moose.

The moose has a sense of smell that, I believe, is unequaled in the animal world. I say this from experience. I have actually touched a wild deer that walked right beside me once. But I have never been able to do that with a moose. Just look at the size of their noses. I do not think that anything can get by them!

Typically, I carry four different scents with me while moose hunting, and they all have their place in my moose toolbox. I carry two bottles of bull-moose urine for when I know I am going to be using a decoy and trying to provoke a bull into fighting, to get him closer to my hunter. I also spray this scent on my head-on-a-stick decoy, and actually set one bottle aside specifically for this purpose. I use the other bottle of bull urine to spray into the air, and to cover my outerwear, when I am trying to persuade a bull to fight.

I also carry a bottle of cow-in-heat urine. If I am cow calling and have a bull coming, I always spray some of this into the air in a fine mist. Not only does it cover the air with cow scent, it also lets me see the air-current direction. Many times I have thought I had the wind in my face, only to spray the urine and watch it flow toward the bull. In such situations, everyone with me gets liberally dosed with the stuff, whether they want to or not. I usually do not give them a chance to say yes or no; it just happens.

I spray my outerwear clothing with this constantly. No matter if I am trying to provoke a bull. A cow in heat drives a bull insane and it is, for the most part, what fuels his desire to fight. Having this scent in the area at or near the time of the rut will never harm your hunt in any way. If a hunter decides to limit himself to only one scent, cow-in-heat urine is the one I would get.

This depicts what can happen when not using enough urine or scent in a large enough area. The bull didn't smell the scent and walked right by the hunter.

I carry a bottle of mare-in-heat urine as well. It has been proven that moose are attracted to female horses in heat, and this urine is collected from female horses that have been injected with moose hormones. Up close it has that horse barn smell. The stuff is relatively cheap as scents go and it does work, so I may use it to keep a bull in an area overnight without it costing me a lot of money. It also makes a very cheap cover scent for the guys that do not take the precautions with their outerwear. If you are the type of hunter who wears his clothes in camp and in the truck between hunts, this may be something that you might want to consider.

The fourth scent that I keep on hand at all times is rather expensive, but I feel that it is worth it. I have seen it work on more than one occasion. A small bottle of bull-moose semen can be indispensable in the right circumstance.

Knowing that bull semen is just that, semen from a bull moose, you can figure out why it is so expensive. It's kind of hard to get from wild animals, and there are not that many bull moose in captivity to be able to produce great quantities of it.

Maryo's first test of the stuff made a believer out of me. He found an area that moose were crossing regularly, although he did not know if they were crossing at night or during the day. He placed the contents of a one-ounce bottle of moose semen on branches in the vicinity and left. Later that day, after legal shooting hours, he drove back by the crossing. Right in the road were two bull moose fighting! His girlfriend, Veronique Levesque, bailed from the truck and got what I think is some of the best footage of battling bull moose that has ever been filmed.

A word of caution when using moose semen: Never get any of it on your clothing. Maryo demonstrated to me what can happen by walking past a bull moose in a pen with the cap removed from a bottle of semen. The bull dropped his head and viciously charged, hitting the chain-link fence hard enough to cause it to flex forward. If a person's clothes gave off a whiff of semen while he or she was decoying a moose, it could turn ugly.

One other type of scent worth mentioning is a combination of food and musk. Buck Expert makes one called Bull Site, a mixture of fermented fruit and plants, with some moose musk and urine blended in. I find that this particular type of product is good to add to an area you are preparing for the next day, and I also like to use it at bait sites prior to the season to draw moose in. I have sprayed Bull Site on vegetation that a moose would not normally eat, and seen what appeared to be evidence of moose chewing on the coated plants, just to get a taste of it.

I may not carry this with me at all times, but I still like the idea of having a bottle back at the truck, so if I do see a situation that calls for Bull Site, I can get it.

SCENARIOS FOR THE USE OF SCENTS

Other than the obvious fact that moose urine is good to cover human scent and alleviate some wariness in an approaching moose, let's look at some of the other times scents should be used.

MOOSE HUNTING

SCENARIO 1: You are calling in the afternoon, just before dark, in an area you know a big bull uses regularly. The wind may be blowing just hard enough that you may not be able to hear any responses you are getting. You lose legal shooting light and you have to leave. Take either the mare-in-heat or the cow-in-heat urine and spray the area liberally. And I do mean liberally.

If you are using mare-in-heat urine that comes in one-liter bottles, half a bottle is not too much. If you are using cow-in-heat urine that comes in 500 milliliter bottles, a full bottle is not too much. I actually plan on one bottle of cow-in-heat urine for each day I am going to hunt. In this situation, it is also a good idea to spray some of the Bull Site mixture in the area as well. It will just be another scent to keep his curiosity piqued.

The next day, as you head back to the last spot you called and sprayed the urine, watch for fresh tracks in the road and pay attention to their direction of travel. If you are like me and have doused yourself in urine, you may find the bull has tried to follow you back out to your vehicle. This has happened to me on more than one occasion.

If the bull heard you and got there after you left, you will likely see where he pawed the ground and wandered around looking for the cow in heat. If you get back to the spot and find that he has been there, follow his tracks and try to determine where he went into the woods. At this point, start your calling. Make sure you sound just like you did the night before. Do not change calls or try a different sequence. Keep it exact. He already knows who he is looking for.

This scenario has allowed me to kill more moose than I can think of. It is my favorite trick to use each and every day.

SCENARIO 2: The day before moose season begins, or on a day during the hunting season, you find an area that has been frequented by a bull moose. There may be some fresh rubs and a scrape or two. You definitely do not want to call to him to find out if he is still in the area. That would tip your hand for the next day.

Liberally douse the area with cow-in-heat urine. Pay close attention to the scrapes. If no scrapes are present with the fresh rubs, make one and apply the cow-in-heat urine to it. Do not be shy with it. Also, liberally apply bull urine to the site.

The bull in the area knows he did not make your scrape. He is not going to like the idea of an interloper in his territory. He has smelled the cow in heat and wants to know where she is. To make the ground I am hunting that much more appealing, I place some bull semen around the area. If the bull is still in the vicinity and catches the scent of all this activity, he is going to come back. I have found that they will hang around for quite some time before getting bored and moving off.

This scenario has played out in my favor on more than one occasion, and I look for this type of situation constantly—especially the closer I get to the actual hunt. If I find an area such as the one described three days prior to the hunt, I will revisit it in the following days to determine if the bull is still there. Once I determine that he is, I prepare the area the night before the season opens, with the anticipation of being back there at daylight the next morning.

This drawing shows why it is wise to use an ample amount of scent and laying it out in a line. The bull finds the scent and then works his way through the area looking for the cow. Eventually, the hunter will get a shot at the bull. If the scent was laid out in the evening and the hunter was not there, chances are the bull would still be near by in the morning and be very receptive to a cow in heat call. Having spent all night looking for this mystery cow, he will want to find her.

SCENARIO 3: Maryo used this little trick to help a hunter kill an exceptionally large bull during a late Maine moose hunt.

The peak of the rut was well past. Bulls were responding to calls, but coming in silently. Additionally, the smaller bulls were the first to show up, being more eager to take advantage of any cow that was still in heat.

Maryo took a bottle of spike-bull urine and a bottle of cow-in-heat urine and sprayed it liberally on the bushes along the trail into the area he was hunting. He used a 500 ml. bottle of each type of urine, feeling satisfied that he would be getting the scent out over a large area no matter what the wind currents were.

Having that gut instinct all good hunters possess about the bull being in the area, Maryo, the guide, and the hunter decided to stay in there all day. Most of the time, the hunting party would return to camp during the mid-day slow hunting periods. While taking a sandwich break at 10 a.m., Maryo heard a twig snap, looked up, and saw the bull they were after. He was coming with his nose held up into the wind and faintly grunting in response to what his nose was detecting.

By covering the area with both moose urines, it appeared to the incoming bull that a young bull was interfering with his females on his territory. Measuring out at over sixty inches, the trophy bull was going to have no part of that.

Maryo told me if the bull had not appeared that day, he would have made sure to go back there the next day. Sooner or later, the bull would have caught the scent and believed that there was renewed breeding activity in the area, which would have triggered his breeding instincts and made him much more susceptible to calling.

One key to most hunters' lack of success when using scents is not using enough. I have seen hunters spray a couple of pumps of urine on an area and call it good. That just isn't enough to grab the attention of a love-starved bull. When I apply scent, I really spray the area!

Remember that the scent is going to be carried by the wind. If you only spray one little spot, the wind will only carry that scent in a very narrow line. If you take the time to spray a one hundred-foot or more swath, the scent will go out over a larger area, which in turn will catch bulls' attention much more readily. The more chance they have of smelling what they are looking for, the more chance you have, as a hunter, to harvest the bull of your dreams.

Spray urine on vegetation that will hold the smell. Look for flowering plants that have dried and have a cotton type of flower, and for look for leaves that are covered overhead by other leaves on another branch—anything that will hold the scent, even through a frost or the sort of light rain that may occur at this time of year.

For the semen, I use another scent holder. I buy some cheap clothesline with a cotton fiber center. I dip pieces of the clothesline in the bottle of semen and then tie them to branches three to four feet above the ground. While this is not a normal height for moose to leave such drippings, it gets the scent out into the air and will pull the bulls in.

I have known a bull to shred a small sapling over night after I had tied pieces of semen-soaked rope to the tree. I attribute this as a to reaction to the smell. The

When I place scent on a tree, I use a piece of cotton clothesline soaked with moose scent.

bull did not like the idea of another bull in the area. He was sexually frustrated from the scent of the cow in heat and the bull semen.

On more than one occasion, after prepping an area, the bull showed up there the very next morning. Once, when I prepped an area the night before we planned to hunt it, we arrived at the site the next morning on ATVs, because I had a hunter who had issues with walking any distance. We drove closer than I would have normally and shut the ATVs down one hundred yards from the prepped site.

Immediately we could hear a bull grunting! We crept down the road and observed him shredding a small poplar tree in which I had tied a piece of semen-dipped clothesline. Other trees were equally destroyed, indicating to me that he had been there a while.

With scents, you cannot be shy with their use. If you only plan on a bottle for an entire hunting season, your best bet is to go without—the reason being that by the end of the hunt, you will walk away from the experience with the idea that scents do not work, when the truth is that most hunters do not use enough to allow them to work! Here is what I plan on for a one-week hunt:

- One 500-ml. bottle of cow-in-heat urine for each day I plan on hunting
- One 500-ml. bottle of bull urine for my decoy
- One 500-ml. bottle of bull urine for every two days I plan on hunting
- A one-liter bottle of mare-in-heat urine for every three days of hunting
- A one-liter bottle of Bull Site for the week

With this planning, I often have scents left over, and I find it best to put them in the freezer. They will stay fresh to keep from one year to the next, and won't have the ammonia scent common to urine that has gone bad. If you opt to freeze scents from year to year, place them in a plastic bottle and leave room for expansion during freezing.

Maryo offers these tips to make your use of urine that much more productive:

1) Store urine out of direct sunlight, preferably in a cooler with some ice.

2) When using urine, carry it in a pocket that has direct contact with your body to keep it warm. Warm urine will smell stronger and be that much more realistic, which can be critical if you are spraying it while calling to an approaching bull. I carry mine in a fanny pack that has separate pockets for each bottle of urine, and use a disposable chemical hand-warmer heating pack in each pocket next to the bottles to keep them warm.

3) A cow moose in heat will urinate up to three to five gallons a day. You cannot over-use urine, so spray it liberally and often. ■

6
DEALING WITH OTHER MOOSE

An an ideal calling situation, you have one bull moose at a time responding to your call, but that may not be the case. More than likely, in good moose country, you will have more than one moose responding to your calls. This can be a help or, more often than not, a major hindrance.

THE YOUNG BULL

A dominant bull will stake out an area, trying to breed all the cows he can. Cow moose are intolerant of other females and will often not allow a rival cow near her bull. That is why a hunter will often encounter younger animals lurking near a dominant bull, trying to pick up any other cows that may be around while the dominant bull is busy with one particular female. I refer to these youngsters as satellite bulls.

Satellite bulls, which may be in the trophy-moose class, will try to get to a cow in heat before the dominant bull does. A hunter will be all but mowed over when a satellite bull responds to a call. But more often than not, the satellite bull will be too young to merit trophy status, and a hunter will choose to pass on him. This is where you run into some problems. A young moose that responds to your call and gets to you before the wall hanger arrives can spell disaster.

SCENARIO 1: The young bull approaches you from a different direction than the trophy moose. Your best bet in this situation is to stop calling, hunker down, and do not move. The dominant bull already has your location and will keep heading toward you, while the young bull is probably going to look for the cow. He may not be grunting at all when he first comes in, but as he looks for the cow that he cannot find, frustration will set in and he will make a grunt or two calling to her.

The young bull grunting is only going to infuriate the larger bull, and may help pull him to your location faster. As long as you do not spook the young bull, you've got the best calling you can get.

Odds are, if the young bull spooks from your presence, he will turn and go back the way he came. Hopefully, he will do it in such a manner that he does not alarm the larger bull. If he blows loudly or acts aggressively, making a lot of noise trying to get out of the area, the dominant bull may get suspicious of you.

That is why it is best not to give yourself away to a young bull. Let him wander around and make his grunts. Chances are he does not want a confrontation with the dominant bull and will pull back on his own.

SCENARIO 2: The young bull is coming from the same direction as the dominant bull, but comes in first. Let him come, even if it means the caller has to pull back from the hunter and keep calling. Drawing the younger bull past the hunter will allow the dominant bull to show himself. The hunter, in this case, must

The caller has pulled back from the hunter. The smaller bull continues towards the hunter while the larger bull makes his way behind the young bull. The larger bull eventually comes in to range of the hunter.

again hunker down and not move. He cannot give away his presence to the first bull if it is not the one he wants.

If the young bull spooks, he most likely will run back the way he came, which is only going to alert the larger bull. If this happens, there's a good chance the larger bull may never be seen. I once blew a client's chance for a bull in this exact situation.

It was daybreak opening morning, and we were walking and calling on a winter road. At different locations during our walk, I would stop and call.

At one location, we heard a response. I put the shooter off to the side of the road so that I would still be able to see him. I moved back fifty feet or so down over a small rise so the moose would not spot me, but I would still be able to see the hunter.

A young bull came strolling up the road like he owned it. The hunter turned to let me know it was not what he was looking for, but I continued to cow call just to see how close I could get the bull. When he finally got what I judged to be close enough, I made my presence known, and he turned and ran back down the road from where he had come. Just as he was about to go out of sight, we glimpsed a nice rack going across the same winter road that junior was running down. The larger bull knew something had spooked the other moose and he was not going to stick his head out to find out what it was. He just knew he had to get out of there.

Two lessons can be learned here. One, do not assume that the first moose you see is the only one there. Two, do not spook the first moose, because he is going to alert the other moose if their paths cross.

SCENARIO 3: If a hunter has two or more dominant bulls coming to a call, it can seem like a dream come true. But being surrounded by bull moose, all on a collision course with you, can often turn into a total disaster!

First off, you are now dealing with more than one set of eyes, ears, and noses, and this is not good—especially if one bull is coming from downwind.

Put yourself in the moose's position and think of it from his perspective: You hear a cow in heat calling. You answer back and so does your competition. You feel you can take the competition, so you continue on your way.

The cow is still calling and the other bull or bulls are answering. All of a sudden, your competition goes quiet. "Hey, wait a minute!" you, as the moose, think. "What happened to him? Why did he shut up? He wasn't even there yet."

The human has just been busted! The other bull, coming from the upwind side, is going to get suspicious. The hunter will need to make a judgment call in such situations, because I have seen a couple of different things happen.

One is that the downwind moose spooks; he shuts up and turns around. The quiet makes the upwind moose suspicious. He now shuts up himself, but the cow in heat is just too appealing, so he cautiously continues toward the sex-starved female. He does not grunt, nor does he rake his antlers. He is searching and, more than likely, will start to move around to get on the downwind side, wanting to smell the cow as well as hear her.

The hunter, at this point, may need to reposition himself if he elects to stay put and see what Mr. Upwind is going to do. In repositioning yourself to improve your field of vision, use the natural land features to determine where the moose may try to circle you.

The alternate ending to this scene is that the downwind moose spooks, shuts up and goes away, and the upwind moose, noting the quiet, becomes suspicious and just leaves the area.

When this happens to me, I usually take the time and try to play out the first scene. Since you have no way of knowing if the upwind moose is going to leave, I find it best to assume he is coming in quietly and cautiously. Sometimes it has paid off, and then again, sometimes it has proved to be a waste of time. But as with any other hunting, you never know. So your best bet is to play it safe.

Once I found a valley in the north Maine woods region that was literally full of moose. I went there every day of the hunt, and each morning we could start four to seven bull moose. We never did kill any moose in that valley; there were just too many of them, and one or more would bust us daily before we were able to shoot. This, in turn, spooked the other moose that were coming, which made it a very frustrating hunt for all of us.

Since that time, we have named the area Frustration Valley, and as of the date of this writing, not one of the guides I am associated with has had any success there; there are simply too many educated moose in this area.

THE COW IN HEAT

This particular moose is the worst nightmare any moose caller can encounter. If you have any experience with a cow in heat, you know you should leave immediately as soon as you hear her. But the thrill and ego trip of trying to break the bull away from her can be overpowering. I know from experience that all good moose callers end up staying put and trying to call her lover away.

Every now and again a hunter will encounter a bull moose with a harem. It does not happen too often, but it does happen. A cow in heat is an extremely jealous creature, and she is not going to let her man leave, let alone look at another female. She will tolerate her bull moose wanting to get closer to hear another cow, but there comes a point at which she becomes more than agitated, and will literally start to beat him up to keep him from straying. If you listen closely, you will hear what is taking place.

A cow that reaches an extreme state of jealousy will actually use her body to steer a bull away from her rival. Depending on how well the male listens to a female, he may turn easily or she may have to use force, such as ramming him with her head.

On those mornings when the air is cold and crisp and the sound carries well, I have heard a cow knock the wind out of a bull by head-butting him in the ribs.

I have more stories about a cow in heat that has spoiled a hunt, and all of the guides I am associated with have similar stories. But Maryo Pepin is the only man I know who successfully pulled a bull away from a cow in heat. Corey Kinney, who was with Maryo when he pulled off this feat, told me he had never heard a cow so mad.

Once, while hunting with a caller from Quebec, we had an entertaining time with a cow in heat. We had been calling a bull for quite a while when suddenly a cow in heat opened up. The bull kept coming closer to us, and the cow was getting more and more agitated the closer to us he got.

This particular Canadian, being the typical moose caller, was looking at the situation as a conquest, the way all good callers do. As he mimicked the cow's calls, he would look at his watch and time her vocalizations, then respond with calls that were as long as hers, with the same tone and pitch. He brought the bull well within one hundred feet of us, but due to limited visibility, we could only see sapling tops moving in the direction of the pair.

The caller finally called "game over" when the cow let out a call that lasted for a full fifteen seconds. He turned, looked at me, and in his broken English announced that his lungs were not that big, and there was no way he could even compete. Finally, hearing the happy couple move off away from us, we had to call it a morning.

I am never exactly sure what to do in this situation, and other guides always give the same lament. Wishful thinking tells me to stay put and hope that I have finally learned to say in moose talk, "Hey big boy, it's better over here with me!"

Hindsight being 20-20, I always think, after the moose has moved off, that I should have taken the hunter into the woods cow calling and trying to stalk in on the pair. I have yet to try that approach, although guides I know all tell me the same thing: "You should have gone after them." Yes, we should have, and some day one of us will. I am sure that we'll have varying degrees of success, depending on wind, field of view, and other factors. I am convinced that it is what the average or better-than-average caller should do in order to score in such a scenario.

I have had a chance to see two different cows in heat with bulls—one in person and the other on videotape. Each episode went pretty much the same, and both are worth mentioning to give the reader some insight into moose behavior.

My first experience as an eyewitness to this behavior was a day before a Maine moose hunt actually started. We were scouting, saw a bull out in a cranberry bog, looked him over and determined that it was not an animal we would want to kill during the hunt. I decided that since he was in the open, it was a perfect chance to observe his reactions and maybe gain some more insight into how moose respond to calls.

I made the cow-in-heat call. He immediately picked his head up, turned in my direction, and started toward me. I was thinking to myself, "Wow, this is going to be too easy." Then, out of nowhere came a lovesick cow. I was so engrossed in watching the bull, I never saw her.

She literally cut off his progress toward us by throwing her body in front of him. As he tried to continue in our direction, she became more aggressive with her body. I would call and he would respond and move toward us. She would call back to me in a jealous rage and force all her weight onto him to thwart his forward motion.

MOOSE HUNTING

I had originally spotted the bull at about two hundred yards away and I got him to come in about one hundred yards. Finally her bellowing and screaming, coupled with her body slams, convinced him that it was probably best if he stayed with her. I watched them walk away together. But he did keep responding to my calls, as did she. He was telling me he'd be back, and she was telling me to go and find my own guy.

The other incident of a cow in heat with a bull went pretty much the same way. Bernard Metivier called a bull out into a winter road for a bow hunter. The bull was over two hundred yards away. As he took a couple of steps toward Bernard and the hunter, out stepped a cow.

That cow would have no part of another female moving in on her man. She walked in front of him and stopped. The bull stopped and did not even try to walk past her. Bernard continued cow calling and the bull refused to attempt to get around the cow he was with, although he shook his head and looked down the winter road longingly in Bernard's direction.

Finally the cow turned face to face with the bull and licked his nose, and he started to indicate that he was going to move off with her. Since there was no way that bull was going to come into bow range, the bow hunter quickly switched to a rifle.

The bow hunter to this day is glad he made the decision. Bernard knew that he was not going to be able to break that bull away from the cow. He also knew from experience that the moose was truly the largest he ever had a chance to get a hunter a shot at. The bull scored 195 according to the B&C scoring system

An observer might ask, "Why not switch to bull calling and try to challenge the bull?" I observed Corey do this once with a large bull and cow he spotted on the Allagash Waterway. It was the time period between our split moose season here in Maine, and Corey knew that no matter what he did, he still stood a chance to get a crack at the bull when our second season rolled around.

The bull and cow were feeding at the water's edge. Corey took a bull moose decoy and started working toward the pair, challenging the male with a bull call as he walked.

The cow was immediately concerned about the intruder and watched Corey intently. The bull just lifted his head and looked at the decoy. Realizing that the decoy had a small rack of antlers, he watched it, but without much regard for the first few hundred yards.

As Corey drew closer to the pair, the bull got between him and the cow, but would not close the distance to accept the challenge. He only made moves toward the cow and herded her off to the shore. Finally, having had enough of Corey's challenges, the bull simply took the cow and himself off into the woods.

That bull was clearly not concerned with a challenge, as he knew that he had won the cow's heart. By challenging the bull with calls, in conjunction with the decoy, Corey had been able to get well within bow range. However, he did not succeed in making the bull close the distance to him; Corey had to go to the bull.

Any scenario involving a cow in heat will start off the same. The decision a hunter makes is going to depend on:

1. The time frame of the hunt
2. How badly he wants the bull in question
3. The terrain and other landscape features that he may have to deal with

Suppose that the hunter gets a response from a bull and the bull approaches. As he gets closer, the hunter hears a cow-in-heat call that seems to be in the same immediate area of the bull that answered him.

The bull and the cow both get closer—and if it suddenly sounds as if they are side by side, it usually means they are. The closer they get, the more agitated the cow will sound, and the more the bull sounds off to the hunter's call, the more agitated she will become. Eventually, her calls will become louder and longer in length.

Assuming the hunter has a good caller, they may be able to bring the bull inside of one hundred yards, or even closer. But what if the hunter still cannot see the bull? What to do? Here is the way I would play it out, given certain conditions.

SCENARIO 1: It is day two of a six-day hunt, and there are a lot of moose in the area you are hunting. The terrain and undergrowth is such that there is no chance of seeing a long enough distance to get a shot without spooking the pair.

In this situation, I would clear out of the area, since the cow will only be in heat for a twenty-four-hour period. It is best to try and come back in the next day or two and hope the bull has not met up with another cow in heat.

SCENARIO 2: It is day two of a six-day hunt. The hunter, or his guide, knows that this bull is definitely one they want. The terrain and landscape may offer a good view of the animals before they spook. Under such conditions, I would go after that bull. Nothing is guaranteed, but it is worth a shot.

I would go in cow calling, and if that did not get me closer, I would switch to bull calling and challenge him. Before bull calling, I would move off to circle upwind of the pair and start calling from there, challenging the bull to at least get him to hold his position so that I might get closer, and hoping to spot him out in the open.

This situation could be made better with the aid of another caller who continued cow calling from the same spot after the hunter leaves to circle with the guide.

The pair of moose will hear the cow still calling. The hunter and guide will know which direction they have to travel in order to head off the pair and get into a down-wind position. Once the hunter and guide start bull calling, the other caller should stay quiet.

Make the bull focus on the hunter and guide who are challenging him. Two-way radios are a great help in this situation, allowing the hunter and guide who are doing the stalking to ask their partner to let out a cow call, so that they can get a new fix on the animals' positions as required.

SCENARIO 3: It is day five of a six-day hunt. You've got nothing to lose at this point! Go for it, as described previously, and take your chances on getting a good shot at the bull.

MOOSE HUNTING

I personally played this one out with a hunter, but it did not work in our favor. The undergrowth that we had to deal with put the bull within twenty feet of us, yet we could only glimpse a portion of his rack and his legs from the knees down. We never got a clear shot, and the moose finally winded us and took off for parts unknown. This is going to happen and there is nothing you can do about it. Chalk it up to "Hunting, Not Shooting." ■

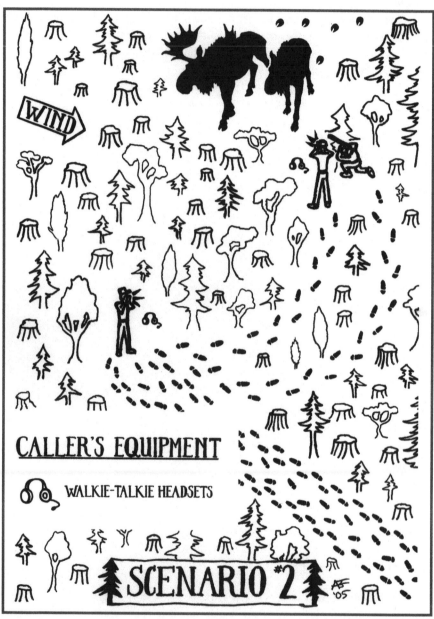

Scenario 2 Cow In Heat. The bull is with a cow and is not allowed to leave her. One caller stays in the original calling spot. The other caller and hunter sneak down wind and call like a rival bull. If all goes right, the hunter will get a shot at the bull.

7
READING A MOOSE'S BODY LANGUAGE AND VOICE

Nothing beats experience when it comes to being able to read a moose's body language and interpret his vocalizations. Unfortunately, most hunters do not have the time to invest an entire season chasing moose around to get an insight into their behavior. Seeing one or two moose during a hunt is not going to give you a whole lot of experience, and one moose's behavior does not necessarily translate into how all moose will act. Moose are not that different from humans; they can get up on "the wrong side of the bed" as well, and that can lead to a bad time, especially if you are using a decoy. No wild animal should be trusted, no matter how much experience you have with its kind.

As I stated earlier, bull moose make two distinct grunts: one that says, "I'm in love," the other that tells a caller, "I want to fight." A hunter must be very aware of these two sounds when calling. It will make the decision about what sounds to use to bring him in that much easier.

The body language of a bull moose will also help you make your decisions. When a bull is agitated and looking to fight, he moves and displays himself in a very predictable manner. He will walk stiff legged with his knees locked, rocking his body from side to side and moving his legs at the shoulder. His head will sway as well. He is trying to show off his antlers, even if he cannot actually see his rival. When a bull can see a rival swaying his antlers, he will match his opponent's sways.

I have observed this when using a decoy. The farther I tipped the decoy antlers to the side, the farther the bull would dip his. One time I had a bull that was twisting his antlers so that they were ninety degrees to the ground. I had to call an end to our showdown when he gave the signal he was going to charge.

Being aware of a moose's body language is an advantage to any hunter, as it will tell you when it is time to shoot or if you need to wait because the animal is going to come closer.

One day, Bernard was calling a bull for a pair of hunters using rifles. The bull, which was coming to his calls with a stiff-legged walk, showed himself at one hundred yards the first time. Although he was well within range of the rifles the hunters were using, Bernard would not give the signal to shoot.

When the bull retreated out of sight, Bernard continued his calling. He knew that the big moose wanted to fight and could be talked into coming back. The bull reappeared and came even closer than before and then, again, he retreated out of sight.

Bernard kept up his calling and brought the bull to within fifty yards of the hunters, at which point, seeing a change in the bull's gait, he gave the signal to shoot.

Bernard and I reviewed the videotape he had made of that hunt. You could plainly see the moose stopped walking stiff legged and took one extra step forward. He stopped at this point staring right at the hunters' blaze-orange hats. That is when Bernard gave his signal. With all the experience Bernard has had with moose, he knew that bull was going to come in looking for a fight. He kept his composure and got that moose as close to his hunters as he felt he could.

Bernard prides himself on providing a good hunt for his clients, and it was apparent that those hunters had a good time. They admitted to me that they had their doubts when the bull retreated the first time, but Bernard told them not to worry; he would get the moose back. He did that, and then some.

Moose, with their poor eyesight, tend to doubt themselves at times. If the wind is in a hunter's favor and a moose stops and stares, it is because he saw or sees something he does not like. He just does not know what it is, and so he waits for one of his other senses to confirm what his eyes suggest.

As a caller, you want to be aware of not only what the moose is doing, but what movements your hunters are making as well. If you notice that the moose abruptly stops and stares at your hunters, it is probably because he caught some movement. If he holds his ground for a second or two, then continues toward you, you are probably safe in assuming you can get him closer.

And if he stops, turns, and stares, you may want to think about having your hunter pull the trigger. That behavior has been the dead giveaway for me—the signal that he is getting ready to put some distance between himself and the hunting party.

Many times the bull may appear confused. He will stop, turn and stare, and start to retreat, but you can stop him one more time with another grunt or cow call. The moose is not going to stand there for long. An alarm has gone off in his head, and he knows things are not right, but he wants to make sure of what he is seeing. Shoot, or go find another bull.

A bull raking his antlers tells a caller that he is frustrated, and it is up to the caller to figure out what the bull is frustrated about. He may smell you, but still wants to believe his ears, which are telling him that he is hearing another moose. He may think he should be able to see the other moose making the calls and cannot. He may have heard calls from other hunters before, and as much as he wants to believe that what he hears is an actual moose, past experience does not allow this.

One year, my party killed a bull early in the hunt. I left the camp and drove up to the next zone to help out another guide. His party had experienced a frustrating two days and had only seen a cow and a couple of spike bulls. Nothing they were interested in taking.

That morning, the guide took the hunters and me to a ridge, where we parked the trucks. We walked down an old logging road with an older cut on our left and a hardwood ridge on our right.

The guide told me that on the other side of the ridge there was a small pond. I checked the air current and found it was drifting directly toward the pond. When I asked if we could get around the water by road and call from the other side, the guide assured me that the bull would be out in the cut and not by the pond. He may have known his area, but he did not know moose.

Reluctantly, I started calling, and sure enough, we heard a bull rake his antlers on the other side of the ridge in the direction of the pond. The air current was going right at him, and experience had taught me that the air would carry our scent straight to the moose. I looked at my cameraman, who shook his head in dismay; he knew I was right. The pair of hunters got in front of me behind a screen of small fir trees. The other guide got behind a hardwood, and the cameraman began filming over my shoulder.

I pulled out a bottle of cow-in-heat urine and sprayed it into the air, well up over our heads, and watched the mist drift toward the raking bull. It was several minutes before we heard another response from him. Although it was nothing more than raking antlers, it was definitely closer to us—not by much, but closer just the same. I asked the guide if he had hunted this bull during the week and he told me not yet. I figured the bull could smell us at that point and it was not going to happen.

I continued to call with no response. I sprayed the cow-in-heat urine in the air again and waited several minutes before we got another raking response from our quarry. Both my cameraman and I knew we were in for a long morning!

For the next one-and-a-half hours, I continued to call and spray an entire 500 ml. bottle of cow-in-heat urine into the air. Finally, we saw the bull at the top of the ridge, but he never made another response, except for raking his antlers.

When we were finally able to see him, he was still over one hundred yards out from us. It was too far to take a shot with all the brush and trees in the way, but it gave us a chance to observe him.

No matter what I did with the call, he would not budge. I had run out of cow-in-heat urine, but I still had my bottle of mare-in-heat urine. I sprayed that into the air and continued my calling. Since there was no real noticeable wind, it took a good three to five minutes for the urine scent to be carried to him by the air currents that were rising with the temperatures. Once he caught the scent, he would move forward ten yards or so at a time, stop again and rake. It was total frustration on my part, as well as his.

The hunters, cameraman and I were all wearing Scent-Lok clothing. The other guide was not, and the moose could plainly smell him. The bull wanted to believe that I was a cow moose; he could hear me and smell a cow in heat, but something was telling him to hang back.

Another hour passed before I got the bull to within thirty yards. I had assumed that was close enough for my rifle hunter. I was wrong, but I will say that I learned a lot from that hunt.

Later, when talking to the guide, he told me that he had found the bull early in the summer and had been watching him. When September rolled around, he committed a cardinal sin and started calling, and he told me that early in the month, he had been able to get the bull well within rifle range, but all of a sudden the bull stopped responding to his calls. It was no surprise to me; I knew that the bull got tired of responding to a cow in heat that was never there.

The guide had educated this moose for his own simple enjoyment. The bull wanted to believe that I was cow, but he had been duped a couple of times and was not going to let it happen again. I am sure that the bull could smell the guide without Scent-Lok clothing, despite the fact that the powerful scent of the cow-in-heat urine made him want to check it out closer. It was no wonder that he only responded by raking. He did not want to give away his presence any more than he had to.

On another occasion, I called out a small bull that my hunter decided to refuse. The bull came in with the wind in our favor. Once he was at our location he milled about looking for the cow in heat he had heard. He finally walked into the air currents that carried our scent to him.

Just like it was scripted, he did the stop, turn, and stare in our direction routine. When he turned again to face the direction he had just come from, and looked again in our direction, I sprayed some cow-in-heat urine into the air. It took a minute or two for the scent to reach him. He was more than close enough for us to witness his lips c urling and his head tilting back to get as much of the scent as he could. He immediately relaxed and turned again to face us head-on.

I took the opportunity to spray some more urine into the air. Before the scent hit him, he was craning his neck forward and licking his nose in an attempt to trap more of the aroma. It was obvious again when the scent hit him, as he once again curled his lips back and breathed in deeply.

The moose and I played this game for about fifteen minutes, with my cameraman capturing the moose's responses to the scent. It was a highly educational experience for all of us.

Since that time, I have looked for the nose licking that a moose will do when wanting to trap more of the scent molecules; it has allowed me to spray scent into the air and play to his senses. Callers are well advised to watch for such subtle body indications and use to their benefit.

Bulls are not the only ones that are going to give off body and voice language that you should be aware of. Cows will tell you a lot as well.

I have already discussed the sounds that a cow agitated by another cow makes, so I will not dwell on that again. But cows are the moose that I now fear the most. When dealing with them, I watch for any signs of their displeasure with my presence.

My first bad experience came with a wounded cow. A hunter had shot her and she ran off. We were tracking her rather fast, as we thought she was dead right handy to where he had shot her. I was in front of the hunter, almost running the blood trail, when she stood up in front of me and came at me with front legs flailing in a high-step fashion. I retreated quickly and the hunter was able to finish her off. Thinking about it afterward did not really bother me. I just chalked it up to an animal's will to live and desire to fight off what was bothering her.

After that, I had a similar experience with a cow that was not wounded. My hunters and I had gotten between her and her calf while calling to a bull. The bull turned out to be one that we did not want to take, and when we stood up to leave the area, we found the cow to our left and the calf to our right.

That cow did not know what we were, but she sure did not like us being between her and her offspring. There were some tense moments that followed, and at one point, I was convinced we would have to shoot her. She came at us with front feet flailing several times. More

This is a cow and calf at the research center in Quebec. The cow may be eating, but note the standing hair on her neck and shoulders. She is clearly not happy. I took this picture just before I left the enclosure.

than once, I was only inches away from her. Finally we had backed up enough that she could go to her calf without us being a threat, and that ended the situation.

Another near-bad experience came while testing the prototype of Renzo's silhouette moose decoy.

Corey and I were on the Allagash Waterway in a canoe, looking for a bull that we could use to test the decoy. We had been out the previous day and had not spotted a bull, so we were anxious to see how effective the new decoy was.

When we spotted a cow and a calf feeding in the water, we beached the canoe a considerable distance from the pair and grabbed our equipment. The plan was for me to work the decoy while Corey filmed over my shoulder through the shooting-stalking hole that is incorporated in the decoy.

At a distance of about one hundred yards, we were all set up and cow called to her. She immediately looked in our direction and saw us. At first, she did not pay much attention to us. The wind was in our favor for the stalk, so it was a perfect opportunity to see how close the decoy alone would let us get.

When we broke inside the fifty-yard mark of her and the calf, you could plainly see the hair on her back stand upright. It was the first sign that something might be wrong, but we totally ignored it.

As we closed the distance on the pair, the cow started to herd her calf toward shore. By the time we were less than twenty yards from her, she was out of the water with her calf and staring us down. The hair on her back was standing upright, especially on the neck and hump.

A few yards later, her ears laid back and her hair stood up that much straighter. I still to this day do not know why, but I stopped and figured that was as close as I was going to get. She then made a sound that, up to that day, Corey and I had not heard before. The best way to describe it is a cross between a growl and a roar. Looking back, neither one of us cared to try to get any closer; we let her walk off with her calf in tow.

Walking back to the canoe, we were both pretty quiet about the experience. While we were stowing our equipment, Corey commented that he did not like the sound she made. I concurred that I had never heard it before, and that it kind of unnerved me as well. She was plainly perturbed over our presence, and we both decided that we would not be doing

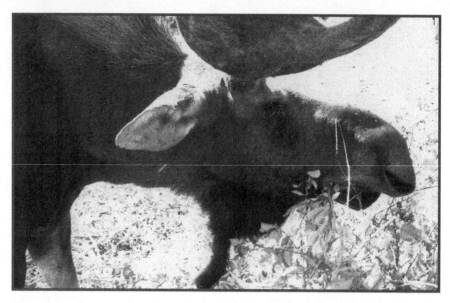

This bull is agitated. Note how his ears are laid back and his eyes are partially closed and rolled back. "End of game" was called before he went into a charge.

that again.

Since that time, we talked to Maryo about that experience, and he informed us that cow moose are the orneriest critters that you will ever come across—especially when they have calves—and he had plenty of stories at his research center to back up that assessment.

My advice to hunters and photographers is to give the cow plenty of distance and watch for that hair standing up. When you see that, it is time to end the game and back off.

In the chapter on decoying, I stated that no one should just get a decoy and head out into the wilds to experiment with it. I highly suggest that you spend some time with a knowledgeable moose decoyer. Even with my experience working with a decoy and seeing it done, I constantly look for the telltale signs that let me know when it is time to call game-over.

Although the head swaying is one key body movement a hunter or guide needs to be aware of when watching or calling a moose, a decoy handler also needs to be looking at the eyes and ears as a moose approaches. One that is going to charge will give you two very important red flags with his eyes and ears:

A moose ready to charge will roll his eyes back in his head; all you will see is the whites of his eyes. He is blind with rage, and his ears will lay back touching or almost touching his neck. If you see either one of these signs, it is time to call an end to the game with him. If you see both of these signs happen simultaneously, you are too late! Your world is about to be turned upside down—literally.

Remember, do not try to decoy moose unless you have been properly trained! ■

SPECIFIC HUNTING SCENARIOS

Now that I have discussed calling, decoys, and the use of scents, it is time to put them all together. I want to share some of the typical scenarios that other guides and I have run across over the years.

SCENARIO 1

WEAPON: Center-fire Rifle
CALLERS: One
HUNTERS: Two
TIME OF THE SEASON: Rut
SCENTS CARRIED: Bull and Cow-in-Heat Urines
DECOY: None
HUNTING LOCATION: Winter road through a cedar and spruce bog that has been cut over. The area has large open expanses with blocks of uncut forest. The regenerated fir trees are three to six feet tall and very thick in places, offering poor visibility if you get off the road.
WEATHER: Clear and frosty at daybreak. No wind is forecast, and the temperatures will reach the low 70s by 10 a.m.

The caller and hunters are walking down the winter road from the vehicle. There is no wind, and the air currents are affected by the lay of the land, with the warmer air rising.

The caller does his calling at intervals of one hundred to two hundred yards apart, and in areas that are open to the left or right. The caller points the call mainly in the direction of the openings. Because temperatures are expected to be too warm to hunt and call effectively by mid-morning, it is understood that the hunt will be fast paced to cover as much ground as possible during the best periods, when sound carries. Waiting ten to fifteen minutes after a calling sequence is going to be the maximum amount of time before moving.

At one of the calling stops, a bull responds with a single grunt. The sound is unmistakable and the direction of the approaching moose is known. The caller softens his sounds and repeats the cow-in-heat call. Again the bull responds at a distance of about two hundred yards away, in an uncut block of trees. He is coming toward a cut-over opening that will allow the hunters to see a distance of about two hundred yards. The cut opening has finger trails that lead off in the direction from which

Illustration 8-1

the moose is approaching. Odds are he will hit one of these trails and work up it toward the hunters.

The bull approaches closer, and as he gets nearer, he can be heard hound-dogging his way up a trail. When a bull is said to be hound-dogging, it means he is grunting with each step he takes, much the same as a hound would when running a track, barking constantly. The caller assumes the bull is less than one hundred yards away; he is still grunting with each step. The caller decides to stop calling and wait. The bull is obviously committed, and there's no sense in taking a chance with a bad note or saying something in moose talk that causes him to "hang-up."

The caller chooses to snap some dried branches over his knee to further convince the bull that he is hearing another moose. As if on cue, the bull comes out on a finger trail into the opening at only fifty yards and stops broadside to the hunters. It is all over!

This is the typical scenario we all want to have played out for us—the easiest of any situation you will ever encounter. (see Illustration 8-1)

SCENARIO 2

WEAPON: Muzzleloader. The hunter should be within seventy-five yards or less.
CALLERS: One
HUNTERS: One
TIME OF SEASON: Rut
SCENTS CARRIED: Bull and Cow-in-Heat Urines
DECOY: Rattling Antler
HUNTING LOCATION: Fresh clear-cut (done that summer) with excellent visibility of up to four hundred yards. Very little new generation growth has occurred yet; there are some small patches of uncut firs and small hardwoods one to three inches in diameter and three- to seven-feet tall.
WEATHER: Cool with temperatures in the high 30s. A wind is already blowing at five miles per hour; it is forecast to reach fifteen to twenty miles per hour later in the morning and expected to last all day—blowing in the hunters' faces.

The hunter and the caller have chosen this cut to hunt because of all the moose sign that is present, and because they sighted a couple of cows there the previous day.

There is a small horseback ridge (the sort of steep rise very common in Maine) one third of the way out into the cut. The hunters can approach the horseback and see the entire cut out in front of them. The distance to the back of the cut is about three hundred yards.

The hunter chooses a location on the horseback, just off the top and with his back to a stump to help break his outline. A few branches are placed to help cover the orange hat required by law without obstructing the hunter's field of vision. He also has a set of shooting sticks all set up and the rifle barrel is placed in them, with the butt of the rifle resting on his knees.

To allow communication with hand signals and head nods to the hunter, the caller chooses to stay nearer the top of the horseback, about fifty feet back and slightly to the right of him. Since the pair has arrived about thirty minutes before legal shooting time, they just sit and listen, but hear nothing.

At legal shooting time, the caller produces a cow-in-heat call. Immediately, a response is heard from a bull at the back of the cut. The wind is making it hard to hear exactly, so the caller holds back his calls to get a better fix on the location of the bull.

The bull sounds off again and appears to be closer. The caller continues with his cow-in-heat calls, occasionally breaking a dry stick over his knee.

The bull continues to approach, but he is coming parallel to the cut inside the tree line to the hunter's right. The bull is only inside the tree line fifty to one hundred feet. The low light conditions only allow for quick glimpses of movement that allow the hunter and caller to observe his forward progress.

The caller begins to spray cow-in-heat urine into the air in a mist. If the wind should shift at the base of the horseback, the moose will get a whiff of a cow. The caller does not want the bull to get behind them and have the wind work against them. He chooses to bull grunt once, followed by antler raking, and also keeps up the cow calling.

The bull stops and answers with his own raking, making his way to the edge of the tree line, still grunting in response. He appears in the cut at a distance of about one hundred fifty yards, slightly forward and to the right of the hunter and caller. The caller is behind a screen of small hardwoods and fir trees. The moose stands and looks for a cow or a bull moose. The caller rakes his antler and makes sure that he shakes the trees he is standing behind so the moose can see the commotion. When he is done with his raking sequence, the caller grunts once using the "I want to fight" sound, with the "click" preceding the grunt. The bull answers with his own fight grunt and continues on toward the hunter's position.

The caller answers with fight grunts, rakes his antler, and even holds it above the tree screen he is behind and moves it, lumbering from side to side. The bull continues to close the distance. The hunter has a "go-ahead-and-shoot" nod from the caller, but chooses to hold fire, as the moose is continuing his forward travel and will only get closer. The caller does nothing at this point. The moose is inside the effective range of the hunter and he knows that once the moose stops hearing responses to his own vocalizations, he will stop and look around, giving the hunter a clean kill shot.

The hunter killed this moose at a distance of less than fifty yards with one shot to the neck from a 50-caliber muzzleloader. The caller allowed the moose to make the fatal mistake of letting his jealousy get the better of him and show himself before he could get downwind of the hunter. As the moose reached the fifty-yard range, he must have thought it a little strange that there were no more responses from either the cow or the bull he was hearing. The bull stopped and turned broadside to look around. That is when the hunter chose to pull the trigger. (see Illustration 8-2)

Illustration 8-2

Illustration 8-3

SCENARIO 3

WEAPON: Bow. The hunter by his own admission wants to be thirty yards or less from a moose to be effective.

CALLERS: One

HUNTERS: One

TIME OF SEASON: Rut

SCENTS CARRIED: Bull and Cow-in-Heat Urines

DECOY: Head on a Stick

HUNTING LOCATION: Dead-end gravel road through a seven- to ten-year-old cut. Visibility out in the cut is limited, as there are many fir trees growing closely together in thick clumps. The moose have trails through this area off to the sides of the road, but the field of vision is too limited to even attempt a stalk.

WEATHER: Temperatures are in the mid 40s. A steady drizzle is coming down and there is no noticeable wind.

The hunter and caller have parked their vehicle at the end of the road and are working their way up the road walking and calling. Sound is traveling well due to the moist air and lack of wind, so they stay in each calling spot for up to thirty minutes listening for a response. Before reaching the end of the road, a bull answers them. He is on the left side of the road off in the woods and coming directly toward the hunter and caller at a forty-five-degree angle to the road.

Once the caller knows the bull is heading for them, he shuts up and backs off down the road from where they have just come as the caller sprays cow-in-heat urine to cover their scent. This will also give the bull something else to clue in on with his nose.

At a distance of about fifty yards from where they expect the bull to enter the road, the bow hunter is placed on the right side of the road, just over the ditch, with his back to a stand of jack firs. Some jack firs are also present to the hunter's right, which will help break his outline. The caller continues back down the road another fifty yards or so away from the hunter and the bull. During this move, he has only made sporadic calls and always made sure to face away from the bull when he was calling.

The bull is continuing toward the road. He has not deviated from his path and will come out on the road where originally planned. As expected, the moose hits the road, stops and looks up and down for the cow he has heard. The caller, standing off to the side, can see the bull, and cow calls to him.

At this point I should note that the bull will make one of two moves. If he hears the cow, he will continue up the road toward the caller, passing directly in front of the bow hunter and offering a broadside shot. The bull should be keyed in on both the caller and the cow-in-heat urine that was sprayed. He probably will not notice the bow hunter at all. If the bow hunter needs to stop the bull for a perfect standing shot, he can stomp his foot on the ground. The moose will usually hear this and stop and look directly at the hunter. The hunter should have his bow at full draw on the animal when he does this. He will only have a second or two to release the arrow.

If the bull freezes in the road and refuses to come toward the caller and hunter, it is time to change tactics. The caller needs to make a bull grunt, shake some bushes, and then step out into the road with the head-on-a-stick decoy, handling the decoy as described earlier. The decoy handler/caller should work slowly toward the bull, making sure that the bull is progressing toward the hunter faster than the caller is—the idea being that the bull has to reach the hunter before the caller does. Sometimes a decoy handler may have to back up instead of going forward to get the bull to come toward the hunter.

The silhouette decoy would work in place of the head on a stick if that were all a caller had to use. If the bull is looking for a fight, the raking antler held over a caller's head works just as well. (see Illustration 8-3)

SCENARIO 4

WEAPON: Bow
CALLERS: Two
HUNTERS: One
TIME OF SEASON: This scenario works well in rut or post rut
SCENTS CARRIED: Bull and cow-in-heat urines
DECOY: Raking Antler
HUNTING LOCATION: Winter road through a spruce and cedar cut.
WEATHER: Frosty in the high twenties. No wind. Midday temperatures are expected to reach the high fifties with bright sun.

Walking the winter road and calling, the party hears a bull respond to their left. The bow hunter is quickly placed into position on the left side of the road with his back to a clump of small spruce trees. One caller positions himself behind the hunter about fifty feet back. The other caller takes the raking antler and goes fifty yards into the woods on the right hand side of the road. It is important to note that both callers have radio contact with headsets. The caller in the woods awaits a signal from the caller with the hunter before making any sounds.

The bull continues towards the road. As he approaches it is easy to tell that he is stopping, sensing something is not right. The caller with the hunter sprays the cow and bull urine into the air. The air currents are such that the bull could be getting a whiff of human scent.

The caller with the hunter keys the mike. This signals the caller in the woods to grunt like a rival bull. The bull again moves in the direction of the road. The caller on the road cow calls and sprays more urine into the air.

The bull steps into the road but his vital zone is obscured by roadside vegetation. The caller with hunter keys his mike twice. This signals the caller in the woods to rake his antler in a tree. Then he grunts once.

The bull takes a step out into the road looking towards caller two and the rival bull sounds. This presents a shot opportunity to the bow hunter. The caller with the hunter calls to stop the bull in the middle of the road, thus giving the bow hunter a perfect shot opportunity. This is a good example of why, at times, it pays to have two callers present during a hunt. (see Illustration 8-4)

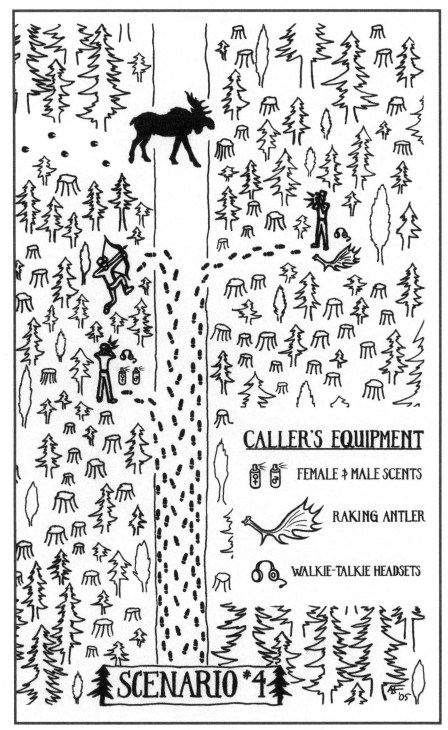

Illustration 8-4

SCENARIO 5

WEAPON: Center-fire Rifle

CALLERS: One

HUNTERS: Two

TIME OF SEASON: Rut or Post Rut

SCENTS CARRIED: Cow-in-Heat Urine

DECOY: Raking Antler

HUNTING LOCATION: Gravel road through a cut-over area. Hunters are traveling between hunting locations in a vehicle.

WEATHER: Temperatures are approaching fifty degrees at mid-morning. There is a slight wind out of the southwest. It has just stopped raining.

The hunters and caller are traveling by truck to another hunting location. A bull moose is spotted running back into the woods, away from the road, in an easterly direction. The caller happens to be driving the truck and he sees the moose at the same time the other two occupants do. He drops a hat from his window and keeps the truck going at the same speed and in the same direction. When the vehicle is a half-mile from where the moose was spotted, the driver finds a place to pull over and park the truck. He and the hunters exit the vehicle, get their gear together, and start walking slowly back up the road to where they saw the moose.

Fifteen minutes have elapsed and the three have walked about a quarter-mile. The caller stops and makes one cow-in-heat call. They wait five minutes, get no response, and continue up the road.

At a point where the caller is able to see the hat that he dropped in the road, he stops the group and makes another call. This time he gets an immediate response from an animal on the side of the road from where the bull was originally spotted. The caller sprays some of the urine into the air to check wind direction; wind will not be a factor.

The hunters and caller all pick a position in a ditch looking into the woods where the bull was heard. The caller continues with his calling, the bull continues to respond, and slowly moves in the direction of the hunting party.

Although progressing slowly, the bull is moving, so the caller must not only keep calling, but also cracking brush over his knee. As an added sound, he rakes the antler in a nearby hardwood tree.

The bull continues moving steadily toward the group and finally makes his appearance at the edge of the road. The hunters wait for him to take another step out and get all four feet on gravel. That simply, the hunt is over. (see Illustration 8-5)

Illustration 8-5

These are the five standard scenarios for a typical hunt during the rut or post rut—five well-nigh perfect hunting situations! You can take each one, change the weapons or the decoys used, and still get positive results. I would like to be able to tell all prospective moose hunters that this is how it will happen. Unfortunately, the perfect scenario does not always present itself. That is why they call it hunting, and not shooting!

Part of the Maine and the New Hampshire moose hunts occur during the post-rut period, and many hunters believe that a bull moose will not come to a call during the post rut. This is far from the truth. I have been able to call moose right up into the end of November. While not all moose will respond positively, a bull that is in the right mood will answer; during the post-rut period, the caller just may have to visit several different areas before finding a responsive moose. But the point I want to make is, with some extra legwork and lots of scouting, you will find a moose that wants to come to your calls.

Moose are no different than other members of the deer family. While the rut may peak at a certain periods, with the majority of the females coming into heat during a given time frame, there will always be a straggler or two that will come into heat later.

Dominant bulls are still going to be territorial during the post-rut period, and they will still try to defend an area from rivals. I have seen numerous bull moose fighting during the month of November—although the fights may not be as violent as during the rut. I have witnessed numerous post-rut battles between bulls where, all of a sudden, they both break off the fight and feed. One of the bulls will get a little ornery and then attack again. It is kind of comical to watch it happen.

The fight will usually end with the more dominant bull chasing the other from the area—a chase that may last for quite a distance. Once, during a November deer hunt, I saw a bull being chased by another. My father had seen the same two bulls earlier that morning, almost a mile from where I was, with the little bull doing his best to get away from his rival.

The key to calling moose during the post-rut period is to play on their curiosity or a dominant bull's territorial instinct. Dan Glidden is extremely successful during the post rut with his soft-calling technique. He cow calls once or twice, and then waits. Dan has unbelievable patience if he knows that a dominant bull is using an area, and will wait in there for hours if he thinks it is worthwhile.

On a post-rut hunt in Maine's zone one, after several other guides from camp had tried all week to bag a particular bull, Dan called in the moose for the hunter by making only a couple of soft cow calls. The two men waited for over an hour before Dan finally saw the bull coming toward them. The bull was grunting back, but very softly. Dan said later that the only way he knew the moose was grunting was to watch its lips move.

Bernard Metivier, on the other hand, takes a more aggressive approach. He covers lots of ground on foot, and stops frequently to call. Trying to provoke a dominant bull by sounding like an intruder in the area, he will usually grunt and rake with his antler or the cone of his call.

Normally, when Bernard gets a response with this calling technique, it happens quickly. The bull will usually be very close and won't like the idea of a rival in his territory. Often the action happens so fast that neither he nor his cameraman has time to turn the camera on to record the events.

The mood of the moose is what factors most in the situation. The more aggressive the moose, the better your chance of getting him into effective range of the weapon you are using. I always tell hunters that the closer they are to the peak of the rut, the closer I can get them to a big bull. The further we get past the peak rut, the harder it is to draw a trophy bull in to that ten- to fifteen-foot range.

I have noticed with post-rut moose that respond to a call, that they will come in silently. By silently, I mean no grunting and no snapping of branches.

On the opening day of a late-season moose hunt, I called in six different moose. The only one to respond with any significance was a very young four-point bull. He came in raking trees, and grunted maybe four times that we could hear.

It was by accident that we actually found the other moose were coming to our calls—silently. My hunters and I were walking a gravel road that had no traffic on it due to a washed-out bridge, and we took a side road off the gravel road that led to a small pond. Walking and calling, we moved toward the pond, and called some more when we got there. Then we decided to walk back out to the gravel road.

We had not gone one hundred feet toward the road when a bull stepped into the skidder trail we were walking—out of nowhere, it seemed. He was too far to get a shot with the bow my hunter had chosen to use, and with the wind blowing right at him on our trip out, he did not stay around long. But I immediately filed that experience away and planned on making it happen again.

Later that afternoon, after we had called for several minutes in a location, another bull popped out on us with no warning. He presented a shooting opportunity, but it was not the animal that the hunter was looking for. The next morning, within sight of the truck, we had a large bull come in silently yet again. The swirling wind prevented us from getting a shot, but it just reinforced what we needed to be aware of.

An hour and half later, another bull of the quality my hunter was looking for showed up to my calls. Again, he made no sound whatsoever as he came. He actually came out behind us, as we had moved forward at a pace that I thought was slow enough. Apparently it was not. We got that moose, however. That season, I learned a valuable lesson about post-rut moose, and the experience has made my subsequent hunts that much more successful.

If a caller thinks there is a bull in the area, and the moose can hear the call, it behooves a hunting party to stay put or move at an especially slow pace, so as to not get ahead of any silent incoming moose.

HANG-UPS

Hunting pressure has a lot of negative impact on how a moose will respond to a call. Animals that are constantly called to, both during and before the season, may start to become call shy.

When Corey and I first started setting up our tent camp in the north Maine woods region, moose were as stupid as they come. It took no time at all to get our hunters all tagged out with trophy moose that they were happy with. Now, after several years of hunting in the same area, we can see that the moose are getting used to being called to. Instead of crashing right in on a caller and his hunters, they have to be finessed into showing themselves. Savvy moose hunters call this hanging-up.

Hang-ups can best be described as having a bull approach and, for no apparent reason, stop short and refuse to come in any closer. Many times, the bulls will be just out of sight. I have had them stop fifty feet from me behind a screen of trees and shut right up. They could hear the cow in heat. They could smell the cow in heat. They could not see it, and the cow did not make any effort to come to them. They simply slipped out of the area away from us with out being seen!

Good moose callers will tell you that for every trophy moose you actually call in for a shot opportunity, they will have another five to seven trophy-class animals that got wise at the last minute and hung-up on them. For every trophy moose that gives you a perfect textbook hunt, figure you are going to work hard to get a shot opportunity at another five or so. I remember one year, in two days of calling, Corey and Maryo started twenty-seven moose. Not one single bull showed himself; every one of them hung-up. It was very frustrating, not only for the hunters, but for the two of them as well. Finally, later in the week, they put to use what they had learned on the first twenty-sevem experiences, and were successful in bringing in some moose for their hunters. Hang-ups are going to happen, no matter how good a caller you may be.

During our guided moose hunts, the callers all get together at night and discuss the day's events. Each caller explains the situations they had, and the other callers offer their insight and suggestions as to what to do the next day, should a similar situation present itself. Oftentimes each caller will tell of the same situation, all the moose hanging-up a certain point in the game. When this happens, it is fairly easy to figure out a game plan for the next day. More often than not, these meetings with all the callers crack the code. The tricks that we all learn from these study sessions often become part of our regular calling repertoire.

One particular year, the bulls were coming to our calls only to hang-up just out of sight. It did not matter if we were able to see one hundred feet or one hundred yards. We were all having the same problem for the first two days, and we all found it of particular interest that the moose would come on a dead run for the first part of their response, closing the distance fast . . . only to hang-up out of sight.

After the second day of total frustration for seven different callers, we came up with this plan: The caller would make a cow call. If a response was heard, the caller would stop calling and run at least one hundred yards into the woods, 180 degrees away from the bull. The hunter would stay where the first call was made. When the moose finally came out, it would be his choice as to whether or not he would shoot that particular animal. Meanwhile, when the caller retreated the one hundred-yard distance, he would call again.

The intent was to make the bull think that he had misjudged the distance to the cow we were trying to imitate. He would then proceed to close the distance, as he had the last few days, but this time he would show himself to the hunter waiting in an opening.

The next morning, three of the seven callers had moose killed by their hunters! The other four saw bulls, and the hunters chose to pass on them.

I used this same trick on a moose hunt in New Brunswick, Canada, with Darrell Richards of Roque Bluffs, Maine. Because the New Brunswick moose hunt is only three days long, you definitely feel the pressure of having to get a moose to show himself on opening day.

Illustration 8-6

On the first day of hunting, all of the bulls we started hung-up on us. The next morning, I used another trick on the first bull to respond—trying to agitate him into a fight—but it didn't work. I then told Darrell and our guide what my plan was for the next moose that responded: I would run into the woods away from the bull for a distance of at least one hundred yards, and continue calling.

That afternoon we got our chance. Not only did we get a response from a bull, we got responses from four different bulls at the same time, all coming from the same area! After the first response, I ran into the woods. At one hundred yards or so from where I had originally called, I called again. The bulls all stopped and grunted back at me. I called again and immediately they all started coming. Coming at a fast pace, I might add. (see Illustration 8-6)

The first bull to show himself to Darrell and our guide was a true trophy moose in the fifty-inch class. He came across the road in front of Darrell at a distance of about seventy-five yards, crossing that road like it was not even there. He showed absolutely no fear of moving through the opening to get to the cow I was imitating.

During another season, we had some of the larger bulls hanging-up on us. They would come to the cow-in-heat call and then stop grunting. We could hear them back in the woods raking trees and walking around, but they refused to come toward us. Bernard was getting particularly frustrated, not being able to actually see a bull despite all the activity.

On the third day, he got a response from a bull. He left the hunter, went back into the woods, and started raking his antler and grunting like a bull that wanted to fight. Instantly, the bull started forward and showed himself to the hunter.

Many of bulls that we called to that week had cows with them. The ones that did not have cows with them when they responded wanted the available females to come to them. However, when challenged by another bull, it was too much for them to take. Fortunately, for some particular reason, the majority of the bull moose we came into contact with that week were fighters.

I have one trick for hang-up bulls I learned quite by accident, and it has worked numerous times, especially true with post-rut bulls. During a morning's hunt, I had started four different bulls. All had hung-up on me at various distances and we never got to see them. It was odd, as they would come hound-dogging toward us, then shut up. I tried some of the tricks mentioned earlier, but nothing would break them free. It was as if we were chasing ghosts.

In the late afternoon, we started another bull. It was going to be the last hunt of the day, so we patiently waited. He was coming toward us at a good clip, and typical of all the others, he shut right up. When he shut up, so did I—more out of frustration on my part than for any other reason. I was out of tricks and just wanted to listen to see if I could hear him moving around.

We had a short walk back to the car, so we waited as it got darker, unloading guns with the loss of legal shooting time. As we stood in silence contemplating the next day's hunt in our minds, out stepped a large bull into the winter road we were on. He had been silent for the last forty minutes, and I think his curiosity got the better of him; he had to come out and see what happened to his cow.

The next morning, on the first bull we started, I talked to him as long as he talked. Once he shut up, so did I. We waited, watching in the direction he was last heard. After forty-five minutes, just as I was starting to think this was not such a good idea, out of nowhere came our bull, silently stepping his way over lay downs and other obstacles. Later that afternoon I called out another bull for another party,

Illustration 8-7

95

using the same trick of just being quiet and waiting him out.

During the 2004 Maine moose hunt, we faced a problem with hang-ups that we had not run into before. We were hunting in zone 11 and had been hunting there for several years. The larger bulls were refusing to come out in the open where we could see them. They would not even cross an opening of significant size that would allow the hunters to get a shot. No matter which of the tricks we tried, nothing would get the big bulls to come out. Plenty of smaller bulls responded to the calls, but the hunters were, understandably, passing them up.

Corey and I discussed this at length and we came up with a plan. We would walk into the area we knew a moose to be and just go into the woods. We would walk until we found a natural shooting lane offering a shot of fifty or more yards. The lane would not have to be exceptionally wide, just clear of branches and trees that would allow a hunter to sneak a bullet through into a moose that we managed to coax into showing itself. (see Illustration 8-7)

Since the moose were hanging-up, we also decided to try a second tactic along with the calling technique. Rather than sound like the cow in heat, and following that by a rival bull call, we would do a cow-in-heat call, then a young bull call, and then a series of agitated cow calls and young bull grunts. It was coming to the end of the week and we had to do something to get the larger bulls to show.

On the first afternoon we tried this, Corey called out an exceptional bull for the hunters. It took close to forty-five minutes from the time of the first response to the moment the hunter pulled the trigger. As Corey said, "It's moose that I work for that I remember the most." And work he did.

Corey started his calling sequence at the edge of a hardwood ridge that rolled down into a spruce growth that had been cut over. The thought we had was that moose had been called to too much from the cut-over area itself, although our normal plan would have been to call within the cut-over area.

Once a bull responded to the cow-in-heat call, Corey kept it up until the bull showed signs of hanging-up—at which point Corey started to grunt like a young bull, mixing, those with his cow-in-heat calls. Once he started doing dual calls he also started walking a twenty-yard circle behind the hunters. He was snapping brush and limbs and stomping his feet, the same sounds an agitated cow would make trying to get away from a bull she did not want to mate with.

All this activity apparently proved too much for the other bull. He came into sight, stepping into the small natural shooting lane they had set up on, and the hunter dropped the forty-nine-inch spread bull on the spot with one shot.

We learned two valuable lessons from this. First, hunting pressure over the years had educated many of the moose in the area. It was time to get out of the major man-made openings and into the woods. Second, we learned that a dominant bull cannot stand the thought of a younger bull getting one of his cows, and he will do whatever it takes to drive the young guy away. Jealousy is a powerful draw to the male of the species, and the downfall of many! ■

9
HUNTING CONDITIONS

Moose hunting occurs at various times of the fall, depending on state or province regulations. If your hunting season happens to be around the time of the rut, be prepared for some warm weather. The rut occurs here in the Northeast at the end of September to the first of October. Days where the temperatures reach into the 70s and 80s are not uncommon.

The first part of the Maine moose-hunting season occurs during the peak of the rut, and then we have another late- or post-rut season. New Hampshire and Vermont's moose hunt usually occurs at the tag end of the rut and extends into the post-rut period. It is still very warm at this time of year. I have had my hunters kill a moose at 6 a.m., when the frost was still on the ground, and before we got the moose loaded in the truck at mid-morning, the temperatures had hit seventy degrees.

The length of time allowed for a moose hunt varies from region to region. For example, the Maine moose hunt lasts six days, while New Hampshire is a little more liberal and allows a full nine days to hunt. The Province of New Brunswick

It was a warm day on this hunt. When packing for a moose hunt, always plan on the possibility of extremes in weather conditions.

has a three-day season, whereas most guided hunts in Newfoundland range from five to ten days, with a six-day hunt being about the average. You can see that your time is limited, and you want to make the most of it to make sure you get your quarry. When you are dealing with temperatures in the 70s and even as high as eighty degrees, you've got to ask yourself, "What am I doing out here?"

As a rule, I tell my hunters that once I start to sweat, we are done hunting. Looking at it from a moose's point of view, I know that if I am sweating, then the moose is dying of the heat and more than likely bedded down in some swamp, keeping cool until evening.

I used to be a hard charger and would hunt all day. Oh yes, on a couple of occasions I killed a moose in the middle of the day, when we were down to T-shirts. But those times were few and far between. What usually happened was I walked into a moose's bedroom and he just happened to be there. He would respond to the call or stand in front of us as we walked through the area. Looking back on it, my hunters and I were worn-out puppies keeping the hours we did. The first year I hunted with the callers from Quebec, it became clear to me that I should quit wasting my time and save my strength for the good hunting days and the optimal times of day.

The first time I hunted with Maryo and members of his pro-staff, I had found an area to hunt before the season started. There were plenty of moose in the area and I felt more than confident. The first morning of the season, my hunters and I were in that area, and we stayed all day. We started a couple of moose in the morning, but when the temperature hit seventy degrees by 8:30 a.m., there was no more response from the bulls. During the day I could get a couple of cows to holler back at me as I called, but nothing else.

The next day, I was fortunate enough to have Bernard accompany us. He had called out a bull with another guide and his hunters the day before, and was looking to get some more footage for his videos. It was the first time I met Bernard and I was looking forward to hunting with him.

I took my party back to the area I had found. Bernard started a bull at around 7:30 a.m. He was looking at his watch as the bull approached, and he kept making these odd faces, looking at his watch and then back at me.

By 8:30 a.m., the bull was definitely making headway toward us, but was still quite a distance away. Bernard looked at his watch and then told me in his broken English that we only had another one-quarter hour and it would be over. I shrugged my shoulders, figuring that I did not understand him. At 8:45, the bull was a couple of hundred yards from us. Bernard looked at his watch and again in broken English told me that the bull was going to be lying down for the day. I knew I understood what he said, but I figured no way was this going to happen with the bull still making progress toward us.

Right on cue, we heard the bull call twice from the same spot. Then all was quiet. Bernard started to gather his gear and pack up his camera. He told me we would come back tonight one half-hour before end of legal shooting time.

I have to admit, I was kind of miffed over this turn of events—having Bernard tell us to leave the area and head back to camp. NO WAY! My hunters wanted to hunt. He said I could go hunting, but he was done until later, and if I wanted to hunt, I should find another place. He did not want any activity in this particular area until that evening.

To make a long story a little shorter, my hunters and I spent the day sweating off a couple of pounds apiece and not much else. Just as he said he would, Bernard met up with us—and proceeded to make things happen from the spot we had been in during the morning hunt! It was just like clockwork. Bernard knew that the bull was lying down and would stay put until evening. Just as the sun was setting behind the trees, the moose got up and grunted, and Bernard returned his greeting.

Later that night, during our "guide's discussion," I got a lecture and an education on how moose work within temperature ranges. Since that time, I have a new philosophy regarding the way I spend my time during a moose hunt.

Here is how a typical day of moose hunting is played out . . .

WEATHER FORECAST: Frost in the early morning. Temperatures will be in the high 20s at daybreak, climbing to the low 70s by mid-day, with bright sun and bluebird skies for the afternoon. Winds light and variable.

3 A.M. Guides are up to get the coffee going and to discuss any last-minute changes they may want to make in their game plans for the day.

3:15 A.M. Guides start preparing lunches for their hunters and making sure they have what they need for a day's hunt.

3:30 A.M. The hunters are woken up. The cook, who has been up since 2:30 a.m., has breakfast started for those who want it.

4 TO 4:15 A.M. Guides are leaving the camp with their parties. Some will have an hour's drive to get to where they want to go. Some just want to get to their area ahead before another party can cut them off and move in.

5 A.M. I arrive with my party at our chosen hunting area one hour before legal shooting light.

5:15 A.M. After finishing one more cup of coffee from the thermos, I put on my Walker Game Ears and walk away from the truck, where my hunters are trying to catch a quick catnap. I walk about one hundred yards from the vehicle to listen for any cow or bull moose that may be calling, looking for a lover.

5:30 A.M. I get the hunters from the truck and tell them to get their gear ready, as we need to move out now. We have a one-mile walk to my first calling spot.

6 A.M. We are at the first calling spot and still have a few minutes to wait before legal light. I do not want to call just yet. A moose could be very close by and show up before we can shoot.

6:12 A.M. Legal shooting light and I make my first call. A bull responds immediately. Anyone who was shivering from the cold is now ready for what is about to take place. The bull keeps answering my calls. Could this be it?

6:45 A.M. The bull finally shows, but he is not what the hunters are looking for. It is only a small bull with a thirty-inch spread. Hey, if this was my hunt, I know I would not take it either. Time to move.

7:10 A.M. We walk to my next calling spot and call.

7:45 A.M. We all thought we heard a bull respond, but apparently we were wrong. Nothing has happened. Time to move. The frost is melting now. I need to shed a layer and hang my jacket in a tree. We continue on our way.

8:10 A.M. We reach the next calling spot. A bull responds. He is behind us. This is not going to work out good. The air currents will take our scent to him before he reaches us. We try to move back down the road to get behind him, and I spray urine as we move backward.

8:30 A.M. The bull hangs-up. He has apparently smelled us, and although he is still calling, he has stopped his forward progress toward us. The temperatures are nearing the high 60s already. He either knows what we are or he is thinking of lying up for the day.

9:10 A.M. The bull has been quiet for the last fifteen minutes. I am wearing my long johns and I am sweating. I need them when we stop to call, but wish I did not have them on when we are walking. The hunters feel the same way. It is apparent that the moose has busted us with the air currents. Too bad, as I know this bull is a good one. Maybe later in the week we can get another chance at him. For now, it's time to head back to the truck.

9:50 A.M. Arriving back where I called once before, we stop to rest. We are all sweating now. I call a couple of times just to see if there might be a bull nearby that had come to my calls earlier. No such luck.

10:25 A.M. The temperature is all of seventy degrees right now in the sunshine. Whose idea was it to walk so far from the truck? We stop and rest and I call again. We get an immediate response from the first bull that we called out.

10:30 A.M. Being as this bull is young and dumb, he comes again to my calls. We all hope that it will be a bigger bull that appears this time but we finally see him. It is the same one we called out earlier.

NOON. We arrive back at camp. On the way back, we checked a couple of other roads for activity, but there was nothing that really interested me. As we pull into camp, I see the trailer gone. "Someone was successful," I say to myself. I see other guides are back as well. No moose in the yard, though. Oh well, we have tonight!

12:30 P.M. Rob, our cook, made lunch with leftovers from last night. I'll eat the prepared meal and save my sandwiches, should we get a moose this afternoon.

1:45 P.M. Time to take a nap. I have heard the news from the other guides who have returned to camp: moose responding, but nothing the hunters wanted to take. The cook tells us that it was, one of the other guides, who came back and got the trailer. His hunters took a nice bull at daybreak. He did not need any help, as it dropped in a road accessible to his 4x4 truck.

3 P.M. Rob comes down and wakes up all the guides who are napping. He tells us that he has hot sandwiches for us before we head out for the afternoon.

4:15 P.M. My hunters and I head out from camp. Ron is still not back with his moose yet. There is some concern, but we know where he is and will go get him if he is not back when we all return.

When Michael Monaco left his home state of New Jersey, I'll bet he only dreamed he would wind up taking such a striking bull moose. This is a bull any hunter would be happy to harvest. Michael was hunting with Newfoundland Big Game Adventures (www.nfbiggame.com).

This dandy bull was taken by outfitter Craig Pomeroy while accompanied by his favorite hunting companion, his sixteen-year-old daughter, Abigail, who has hunted with Craig since she was four years old. The moose was harvested at Craig's lodge, Hinterland Outfitting Ltd. (www.newfoundlandbiggamehunting. com).

Steve Pruit of the state of Kentucky took this good seventeen-point bull while bowhunting at Ironbound Outfitters (www.newfoundlandmoose.com).

Steve Cushing of South Hadley, Massachusetts, killed this heavy-beamed bull with a one-shot Thompson Center rifle at Kindens Quinn Lake Outfitters (www.kindensoutfitters.com) in the fall of 2013.

Holy moose rack, Batman! This remarkable bull was taken in Newfoundland during the 2013 season by George Simpson while hunting with his dad Zack. George and Zack are from California. The antler's overall mass, long points, and tall, wide, and heavy paddles are enough to make any moose hunter's blood flow with excitement. The big bull was taken at Red Indian Lake Outfitting & Tours (www.redindianlake.com).

Ralph Somma of Colts Neck, New Jersey, killed this bull at Arluk Outfitters (www.arlukoutfitters.com) on his first moose hunt and his first trip to Newfoundland. The moose was called in to forty yards by Ralph's guide, Randy. It was taken with a .308 loaded with 150-grain XP3 bullets.

4:45 P.M. We check one road for recent activity. There is nothing that really excites me. I am going to stick to my original game plan and go to an area where I have killed before.

5:15 P.M. We arrive at my calling spot. I make one long, plaintive cow-in-heat call. Time to take a nap.

5:30 P.M. I make another call. Listen . . . nothing!

5:35 P.M. A bull responds in the distance. Oh damn! Now I've got to get him here before it gets dark.

5:50 P.M. I persuade the bull to show himself. He actually comes to us on a dead run, and I get him to within twenty feet of one of the hunters. We all wish he were bigger. He has a forty-inch spread, but no palms at all—what we like to call a Boone and Crockett spike-horn bull. I am sure that in a couple of years, he will be a trophy. It's getting dark so we head back to the truck.

6:30 P.M. Rob has dinner ready. Not all the guides are back, but we eat anyway. It has been a long day and another looms in nine hours. Ron is back with his moose and it is a good one. They have it all tagged. Tomorrow they will take it to the butcher. We all sit and listen to the story of how they got it.

7:30 P.M. Most of the guides are back. We all wander outside at various times to discuss what we saw during the day and, perhaps, what we should do tomorrow. Some of the younger guides are starting to second-guess themselves and are looking for advice. The older, more experienced guides tell them what they need to know. It is not a bad day. One guide has killed and another is still out. Everyone else has had some form of response from bulls and the excitement level is high.

8:30 P.M. Some of the guides and hunters who have returned are drifting off to bed. Another of the guides, Rick, is still not back yet and some of us are getting concerned. Rob places dinner on plates and covers them so that they can be reheated when the missing group finally returns. He has to be up at 2:30 a.m., so he needs to get some sleep.

9:00 P.M. It is decided by those of us still up that if Rick is not back by 9:30, we will go looking for him.

9:10 P.M. Rick and his party arrive at camp. They are quite excited. They have a big bull down. Rick has taken care of it. The hunters really want to get it out of the woods tonight. I have stopped questioning their thoughts after all these years. If they want it out, we will go get it out.

9:45 P.M. Rick and his hunters wolf down their dinner. The guides that are still up and a couple of hunters who heard all the commotion when Rick pulled back in to camp are awake. While he and his hunters eat, we gather the gear that we will require to get his moose out of the woods. Even Ron, who got his moose out with only his hunters, is going along. All of us guides pitch in this way, because we know that we will need the other guides' help eventually. None of us wants a black flag hanging over his head.

12:30 A.M. I am the first to arrive back at camp after having helped Rick and his hunters get their moose out. I need to get up in two-and-a-half hours. God, I love moose hunting! Rick and Ron have both said that they would take someone's party in the afternoon in return for the help that they received tonight. Ron needs to get his moose to the butcher and Rick needs to get his tagged and to the butcher. They will be ready to go by afternoon.

So goes a typical day of moose hunting. One can see where sleep is at a premium by mid-week.

Different weather conditions will determine how your day plays out. A weather forecast that calls for dark skies with a steady or off-and-on drizzle is going to mean hunting all day. Moose move in this type of weather. I always tell my hunters to bring good rain gear. If it rains with little or no wind, we are going to hunt.

Rain and drizzle are among the best weather conditions for hunting because the temperatures are normally on the cooler side. Able to move around comfortably, the moose take full advantage of these conditions. Your scent will tend to be washed away in the rain, which makes getting close to a bull a little easier. Additionally, sound travels well in the damp air. Calls will reach out even at midday, and you will be able to hear the moose's response easier as well.

I will hunt on days when the wind reaches gale proportions, but you can bet I am not going to call in my best areas. Moose are like deer in that when the wind blows hard, they tend to lay low and not move around much.

You can call moose in windy conditions, but you never hear them coming in.

Hunting with snow during the rut can be different. Remember to include scents and moose calls, as they can make all the difference between a successful hunt and one that's not.

The following images were provided by Newfoundland and Labrador Outfitters who are all licensed members of the professional organization Newfoundland and Labrador Outfitters Association (NLOA). Visit their website (www.nloa.ca) for a complete listing of member outfitters who specialize in providing guided hunts for moose from their lodges. I want to thank both NLOA and each individual outfitter for their time and interest in providing these images for this book.

This huge twenty-two-point bull was taken by Alex Crosbie in Newfoundland, Canada. The bull's antlers were fifty-six-and-a-half inches wide and were scored by Safari Club at 398 5/8 inches. The moose was taken by NLOA outfitter member—Arluk Outfitters (www.arlukoutfitters.com).

Janice Gunthers took this terrific bull while hunting with her husband Bill, who also got a dandy bull. Note the long tines and wide paddles on the bull. The Gunthers were hunting at Ray's Hunting & Fishing Lodge (www.huntnewfoundlandmoose.com).

Bill Reisinger of Massachusetts took this fine-looking bull at Moose Valley Outfitters (www.moosevalley.com). The bull's antlers have excellent tine length, width, and paddles.

Ed Krzanowski of the state of Connecticut took this magnificent twenty-four-point monster while hunting with Next Ridge Outfitters (www.nextridgeoutfitters.org) in their "trophy moose location." There's not much left to say about this bad boy other than WOW!

After a long stalk across a huge bog, my guide Dennis Pilgrim noticed the bull bedded down with a cow and a calf. We waited in a thick patch of Tuckamore trees for a few hours before the moose got up to water at a pond. One clean shot from my .270WSM loaded with 150-grain XP3 took this terrific eighteen-point bull down in his tracks. I was hunting at Tuckamore Lodge (www.tuckamorelodge.com).

Often they just appear out of nowhere. Think about this: You have a hard time hearing sounds in the wind and determining where they come from. A moose is no different.

If I get a windy day during a hunt, I stay away from my best areas and do more road hunting, with short walks. If I see other signs that game is moving, I might work into my best areas.

Bernard put it best during the 2004 season, while hunting Zone 13 in Maine. I took him and my hunters into a very good area on day two of the season. The wind was blowing at gale force. Bernard walked into the area, took one look at it, and backed out without making a sound on his call.

The area was too perfect, he explained, and he did not want to be calling moose and not be able to hear the responses. Like he told me in his best broken English, "I call. I no hear the bull rake. I no hear him break the branch as he comes. We leave and come back on next best day."

We came back the next day and used Bernard's bag of tricks to pull a fifty-two-inch bull out into the clear-cut.

There is a saying among true Mainers, "If you don't like the weather, wait a minute." I take that even further: "If you expect sixty- to seventy-degree weather, pack your snowshoes!" One year during our moose hunt, we had a substantial amount of snow. It happened during the rut and it was quite an enlightening experience.

The first morning after it snowed, moose were hard to come by. Some guys did score that morning, but nothing really happened until the afternoon, when the weather stabilized. By the following day, the moose were back to their regular habits and everyone had a great morning.

I cannot say for sure, as I have not had enough experience with such conditions during the rut, but the snow seemed to confuse the moose. They stayed bedded most of that first morning after it stopped. The hunters who did score actually shot their moose while they were bedded down. Just something to keep in the back of your mind should you ever encounter a freak snowstorm during the rut.

Contrary to popular belief, post-rut moose will, and do, respond to calling. I have heard many guides that I considered good woodsmen to lament the fact that by the first or second week of October, moose do not come to a call. Nothing could be further from the truth.

If moose stopped responding to calls, then how can you explain the fact that Maryo consistently calls in his largest moose of the hunting seasons during the second week of the Maine hunt? It's the same for Dan Glidden. Danny always gets stuck working in the toughest zone in northern Maine, and always gets his client a moose by calling.

Post-rut moose are not going to come with the aggressiveness of a freight train, like the rutting moose do. The bulls that come to your calls are going to sneak in on you, often coming in silently. They also are going to respond to different stimuli. Rather than a cow in heat, you may have to provoke them by impersonating another rival bull. Good callers can call moose from September first until the end of November in Maine. The key is being a studious caller, and knowing what to do when you finally get any kind of a response.

People who are booking a moose hunt need to put all their faith into the guide or outfitter they have chosen, and I know it is a hard thing to do. You have laid out lots of money for a hunt. You expect your guide to be able to produce a moose. Every guide I have ever met wants to do that. It does not matter if the guide is from Maine or Newfoundland; they all want their clients to take a moose.

Hunters need to realize that if their guide says take nap, take a nap. If he says that you need to leave at 3:30 a.m. to get to his best spot, be ready to do that. Your guide does not want to be putting in extra hours just to make you think he is working. During a week's hunt, you could very well get a day of bad weather, which is a day of good moose hunting. If you hunt hard all day during hot weather against the wishes of your guide, you may very well be dead tired and not be able to get out of bed to put in a productive day of bad-weather hunting—and it could be the best moose-hunting day of the week. Listen to those who know.

Bernard actually carries hammocks along for his hunting parties. If it is too far to come back to camp for a nap, he simply sets up out in the woods, stringing the hammocks between trees so everyone can take a nap in the heat of the day.

Now, there are some exceptions to these rules. Corey and I have one guide working for us who will only guide in a couple of zones that he knows intimately. He will hunt there all day, focusing on bedding areas during the heat of the day, comfortably spending his time hunting rather than napping because he knows the regions so well.

In the past, I have had hunters who were on a limited time schedule and have had to hunt all day on days that were not conducive to it. Being under pressure is not my favorite way to hunt, but I will if I have to.

Use your hunting time wisely during hot weather. Be where you need to be before first light. Call it a day when the heat starts affecting you, and be ready to go again in the evening one hour before last light. If it rains, plan on hitting the brush hard all day. If you are employing a guide, heed his advice. Be prepared for those long days, and make the most of the short ones. ∎

10
SCOUTING FOR YOUR HUNT

If a person decides to hunt for moose on his own, he should plan on doing some scouting before the season. Scouting for moose-hunting areas involves a lot of driving around and getting out of the vehicle and doing some walking. Even though moose are heavy animals, on hard gravel roads they may not leave much sign that will be visible from a vehicle.

Every year I hear from prospective clients, and the letters or emails go something like this: " . . . we have our moose permit. We have hunted deer in Maine for the last ten years. We see many moose each fall. Our plan is to arrive on Saturday and spend Sunday scouting areas we know of. We hope to have our moose by Wednesday. If we do not have our moose, could you please forward us a phone

number where you can be reached. We may or may not require your services." Spending one day scouting, the day before the season, is not what I would call good time management for what could be a once-in-a-lifetime hunt.

From late summer until the end of deer season in Maine, I am in the woods daily. I start to see moose from the first day of bear baiting right up until I am done deer hunting in November. Where I see moose in July and August is usually not where I see them during the moose hunt. And I can tell you from experience that where I see moose during the deer season is not where I find them during the rut.

Bernard stands in a moose bed in a winter road. Note how the bed is circular in shape.

This is a fresh rub on an alder clump. The broken stalks and the width of the damage indicate a decent size bull made this.

Depending on the time of year, moose have different needs. During the hot dry summers, you will find moose on almost every waterway. In November, you will find them in key feeding areas bulking up for the upcoming winter months. I see many moose on hardwood ridges at this time of year; I am not going to put a lot of time into hunting hardwood ridges during the rut.

During September and the first part of October, I find moose in what I like to refer to as breeding areas. You might ask, "What is a breeding area?" All I can tell you is that it is an area where moose congregate during the breeding season each year. There seems to be almost no common denominator in determining a breeding area, but I can tell you this: When you locate one of these areas, you can go back year after year and find moose present.

I have one such area that I have known about for years. My great-grandfather hunted there back in the early 1900s. Today the area is cut over, gravel roads run through it, and it still holds moose every year. In recent years, we have located a trail that the moose use and we have called out many bulls from the exact same spot over the years. It is almost a guarantee that we will be able to start a moose and get him to show himself right there.

One year we called out a sixty-one-inch bull on Monday and a forty-two-inch bull on Tuesday. Both moose came to us using the same trail and stepped into the road at the same place. If you can find such an area and keep it to yourself, you will not have to do much scouting.

Since I spend so much time in the woods, as do the other guides that I work with, scouting is an ongoing activity throughout the year. The average moose hunter with limited time does not have this luxury.

If you decide to hunt moose on your own in an area you are unfamiliar with, ideally you should have the week prior to the hunt to do your

This maple tree was rubbed the previous year by a bull moose. Finding sign like this during a summer scouting trip will give you a good idea of where to hunt when the season opens.

scouting—which gives you five to seven days to locate where moose may be congregating to breed. It also gives you a chance to perhaps observe the size of the moose that are in the area.

If, like most hunters, I did not have that much time to put into a hunt and had only limited time to scout, I would much rather use my time during the summer months, riding around and observing old sign from the previous year.

Bull moose, like other members of the deer family, make their presence known in an area through scrapes and rubs. The scrapes may be hard to spot in the summer, but the rubs will still stand out, even to the untrained eye.

It has been my experience over the years that moose are lazy creatures. They tend to walk the path of least resistance if not pursued or alarmed, and often old logging roads and skidder trails serve as their main highways.

Bulls rub their antlers on trees, marking their territory. These rubs or "hookings," as they are also known, are normally done on small saplings or clumps of isolated alders. Depending on the bull's aggressiveness when he makes the hook-

This is a moose scrape during the peak of the rut in Maine. It is a large, muddy, musky-smelling area where bulls will kneel or lay down in it during the peak of the rut.

This winter road was made after the ground was frozen, so there is no gravel. These types of roads are ideal for walking and getting away from hunters who post near logging roads.

ings, he may tear up the trees. Sometimes it is just a branch or two broken off; other times, I have seen where bull moose literally shredded a tree, leaving nothing more than a stalk. This sign will be visible from year to year, and it is what a hunter wants to be looking for when scouting during summer months.

Many times during the off-season I have found tote roads that were literally ripped to shreds from past ruts. Going back to these areas prior to the rut, there would be no significant amount of fresh sign. Going back during the rut, the sign showed that almost every moose in the region had relocated here.

A typical breeding area will have a stretch of road or a relatively small area in the woods that is torn up with hookings. If you look closely at the hookings, you will see that more than one moose has used the site.

The height of the rub marks is a clear indication as to the size of the moose that made them; the higher the rub marks, the larger the antlers. Oftentimes individual moose will prefer to rub on one type of tree over another, which will tell you something about their habits. I have seen moose that preferred to rub on fir or spruce trees, which causes their antlers to be a dark brown in color. Another moose in the same area might prefer to rub on hardwoods, such as poplar or alder, which would give his antlers a white or light color. If you are fortunate to be able to put in some scouting time and glimpse the animals, you might be able to observe the antler color of individual bulls.

When the rut starts to come into season, a hunter will observe that young bulls begin to show in an area first, along with the cows. A young bull is feeling his oats for the first time or two. He may not have had a chance to breed in the past couple of years, due to his low status in the hierarchy, but he still gets the urge and will try to be around to take advantage of the first young cows that come into heat.

If I find an area that has a lot of cows and young bulls showing early, I make sure that I get back there the closer it gets to the rut. The big bulls are sure to move in.

When I am scouting, I actually do not like to see the big bulls; I want to see their sign in the form of hookings and tracks. But what I really want to see is some young bulls and an abundance of cows. The abundance of cows is the critical factor.

Many times a hunter just learning to call moose wants to practice his skills in his scouting, but I would advise against this for a couple of reasons.

I have found over the years that I can call my first moose of the year on Labor Day Weekend here in Maine, and every time it is a young bull that responds. As stated earlier, young males want a chance to breed, and they will respond even though the time is not right.

A hunter who goes in calling before the rut and sees nothing but small bulls might dismiss the area as having only small bulls, when the truth is that he may have found an excellent hunting ground. It just so happens that only the youngsters are present early.

As the rut draws closer, you may have an overwhelming desire to go out and try your calling technique. I know; it happens to me every year. But if you go and call a bull in to you before the hunting season, he will be that much harder to fool during the hunt. Turkey hunters tell me they have the same problem with hunters calling turkeys before the season opens. I honestly believe that moose file away the tone and pitch of individual calls; if they came in and found no cow, it's that much harder to call them back a second time with the same calls. If you feel you need to go and practice your moose calling before the season, do it in an area that you will not be hunting.

Occasionally a guide or hunter will have to call during scouting trips to help gauge what stage of the rut has been reached. If I have to use my calls prior to the actual hunt, I do so sparingly, and this is how I do it:

I get on a piece of high ground at daybreak or just at dark and make one short series of cow-in-heat calls. If I get a response, I immediately leave the area and stay quiet. I do not want to tip my hand to a potential trophy; I just want to hear him and then get out of there.

I take the same precautions with my clothing as if I were hunting. If a responding bull does happen upon the spot that I called from, I do not want him knowing it was a human that duped him.

Another problem that limited scouting time will not uncover is the number of other hunters who have discovered the same area. If you limit your scouting to only one or two days prior to the season, you won't to want to spend time going back

This heath is a great place to spot moose. A good moose caller using decoys will get a moose within range in this wide open space.

into areas you have already been in. By giving yourself more time to scout, you can go back to places you scouted previously that showed promise and see what other traffic may be there.

I have a heavily hunted road near my camp, and I know everyone and his brother hunts that road. It literally has tire ruts in it after the first week of moose hunting.

One year, the day before moose season started, I took my clients into the area just to show them a moose. We saw three bulls that evening, and the clients were all excited to go there the next morning. No way was I going there. I knew there would be a considerable amount of traffic in the area and it would make calling next to impossible.

As it was, another party I knew was hunting across the river from that particular area the next morning. They informed me that after first light, it sounded like a small war had started there. We later found out that only two small bulls had been taken that opening morning, in the same place where I had shown my clients three bulls the day before. Another acquaintance of mine who actually hunted the area on opening morning said that a traffic light could have been put to good use at an intersection.

MOOSE HUNTING

When I took my clients in to the area on Sunday evening, we knew that others had found the place, but we never saw another vehicle. It has always been the case with that particular road system, from the day it was built.

Another time, I was going through the motions of scouting an area I hunt every year—a road system that, in the past, I had always had to myself. On my first day of scouting, I did my customary drive through and saw several other vehicles that I knew were scouting for moose. It kind of bothered me, but I let it go.

During the next day of scouting, I drove into the same area again—only to encounter some of the same vehicles from the previous day, and a couple more! On the third day of scouting, after another drive through, I knew my secret was out, and there was going to be too much competition in the area. I decided to blow it off and find a new place to hunt. Luckily, I had other areas in reserve, so I did not lose any sleep over losing my once-private hunting ground.

Had I only a limited amount of time to hunt and not known the region, I would have wasted a considerable amount of time trying to hunt in all that traffic. Constant use of a road system is not conducive to good calling, and it makes for a very tough road hunt. The moose just get so riled up at the new traffic patterns, it puts them on edge.

If you are going to hunt for moose on your own, do yourself a big favor and allow plenty of time for scouting. The rewards far outweigh the costs. ■

11
HUNTING ALASKA'S GIANT BULL MOOSE

If you ever daydreamed of hunting some of the world's largest bull moose, you should consider hunting in Alaska. Be sure your moose hunting expectations of Alaska hunting are realistic, however. Moose are not behind every bush in the fiftieth state. Alaska also has complex hunting regulations and land ownership rules in some areas that hunters need to be aware of. With that said, moose hunting can be amazingly good in Alaska. Although moose aren't behind every bush, their populations are dense enough to make for very good hunting prospects.

Heavy-bodied and long-legged, Alaska's moose are the largest in North America. A full-grown (mature) bull can stand six feet high (or slightly more) at the shoulder. Mature bulls that are in prime condition often weigh between 1,200 and 1,600 pounds! Adult females are somewhat smaller and generally weigh from 800 to 1,300 pounds. A 1,600-pound moose will field dress out at about 950 pounds, yielding approximately 500 pounds of edible meat. Alaskans and non-residents annually harvest 6,000 to 8,000 moose, which translates into about 3.5 million pounds of one of nature's most tasty big-game animals (see the chapter on moose recipes).

As mentioned in other chapters, the largest moose antlers in North America come from Alaska, the Yukon Territory, and the Northwest Territories of Canada. Trophy-class bulls are found throughout Alaska, with the largest antlers and body weights coming from the western portion of the state. Generally, bull moose will occasionally grow a trophy-size set of antlers when they reach six or seven years old. A bull may be ten or twelve years of age before it grows its largest set of antlers. According to the Alaska Department of Fish and Game, wild moose "rarely live more than sixteen years." It is not uncommon in Alaska for a mature bull, particularly one who has reached ten years old or older, to have antlers that are seventy inches wide or more.

Moose in Alaska occur in nourishing habitats from the Stikine River of Southeast Alaska to the Colville River of the Arctic Slope. Moose are most plentiful in areas that have recently been burned and that contain willow and birch shrubs, on timberline plateaus, and along the major rivers of South Central and the interior portions of Alaska.

BIG-GAME LOCKING TAGS

Nonresident hunters must buy appropriate locking tags to hunt big game in Alaska. This tag is locked on the animal immediately after it has been killed and must remain there until the animal is processed or exported. In addition to a hunting license, some resident hunters must buy a brown/grizzly bear locking tag or a muskox locking tag when they are hunting these species. It is recommended by the Alaska Department of Fish and Game that both resident and nonresident hunters refer to the Alaska Hunting Regulations when they are planning a hunt in order to determine if they need a locking tag. All pertinent hunting (and other) information about moose hunting can be found on the Alaska Department of Fish and Game website at www.adfg.alaska.gov.

Moose are among the most popular big-game animals to hunt in Alaska. As I have often found, no matter where hunters stalk moose, many are surprised at how large a bull moose is. This is particularly the case with the Alaska bull moose. A mature animal can weigh up to 1,600 pounds, stand over six-and-a-half feet tall at the shoulder, and carry a huge set of antlers that generally exceeds sixty to sixty-five inches—sure to astonish anyone, especially a novice hunter.

Where to Find Them: There are twenty-six Game Management Units (GMU) within the state. Moose in Alaska can range from certain areas of the Inside Passage all the way north to the Colville River area in the Arctic. They are particularly common in cities like Anchorage and Fairbanks during the winter months, when tender shoots and leaves are hard to come by in the wild because of deer and snow.

Some of the state's best moose hunting is found in Juneau and surrounding areas. The south-central portion of Alaska is more varied, however. This region begins at Icy Bay on the Gulf of Alaska. Moose in parts of south-central Alaska are currently among the most numerous in the state, especially in the Matanuska and Susitna valleys. Nevertheless, good populations exist in suitable habitats throughout the region. For more general south-central Alaska hunting information and regulations contact the Alaska Department of Fish and Game, Division of Wildlife Conservation, 333 Raspberry Road, Anchorage, AK 99518-1599, or call (907) 267-2347.

Moose (and caribou) are the most visible big game in the interior, and in the Arctic and Western Alaska areas. These regions encompass the huge area drained by the Yukon and Kuskokwim rivers and draining into the Bering Sea, Kotzebue Sound, and the Arctic Ocean. This is relatively dry country, and habitats vary from the forested interior to the western and arctic treeless tundra.

For interior Alaska information contact the Alaska Department of Fish and Game, Division of Wildlife Conservation, 1300 College Rd, Fairbanks, AK 99701-1599, or call them at (907) 459-7313.

For western and Arctic Alaska information contact the Alaska Department of Fish and Game, Division of Wildlife Conservation, Pouch 1148, Nome, AK 99762, or you can call (907) 443-2271.

For general Southeast Alaska hunting information and regulations information, contact the Alaska Department of Fish and Game, Division of Wildlife Conservation, PO Box 240020, Douglas, AK 99824-0020, or contact them by phone at 907-465-4265.

Season Dates: Wildlife packages arranged by knowledgeable guides are the only way in my view to hunt moose consistently successfully in Alaska. There are countless guides and outfitting services available in Alaska and accommodations range from tents to five star lodges.

Outfitters can reach their lodges in a variety of manners including float plane, boat, horseback, ATV, Argo, or helicopter. Hunting can be done on foot, on horseback, by boat on floating waterways, or by a variety of all-terrain vehicles.

However, in some parts of the state moose-hunting regulations require that a bull moose have up to four brow tines on at least one side and/or fifty-inch-wide antler spread to be legally taken by hunters. While this regulation helps provide for some immense bulls, and more opportunity to take world-class trophy moose, it also demands that hunters carefully look over a bull's antlers to make sure the bull is legal to shoot.

THE ACTION

Like in almost all other areas of North America where moose are hunted, the primary hunting tactic is using moose calls (vocalizations made to imitate both receptive cows and rutting bulls) along with raking brush, snapping twigs, and even "pawing" the ground. Another strategy that is used in Alaska is spot-and-stalk hunting. As any seasoned, reliable guide in Alaska will confirm, big bulls aren't waiting around standing in open terrain. A hunter has to be willing to hunt diligently and have patience in order to get a good mature Alaskan bull moose. The action can get intense (up close and personal) wherever you hunt moose, but in Alaska, a close encounter with an old bull-moose can mean a change in underwear. Guides I have talked with have told me that the average shot in the state is at a distance of thirty to seventy yards—and often closer than that. About 65 to 70 percent of Alaskan nonresident hunters use a firearm and the balance use a bow.

When calling a bull in rut he can be inflamed, agitated, and short on good temperament. Again, while this is true about bull moose anywhere they are hunted, in Alaska their sheer size requires an extra amount of extreme caution whenever you call. A fully mature rut-crazed bull moose is dangerous. They can cover an amazing amount of ground faster than most hunters think bulls can. Like in many Rocky Mountain states, particularly in places that border Yellowstone Park in Montana and Wyoming, grizzly and black bears have come to connect an elk call or even a gunshot to an easy meal. The same holds true in Alaska: big brown bears and black bears can associate moose calls and brush raking as a lunch opportunity. When calling and raking in Alaska, stay alert and be prepared for anything that shows up when you call.

Alex Crosbie poses with a huge Eastern moose he took with NLOA member Arluk Outfitters.

12
MOOSE HUNTING THROUGHOUT CANADA

majority of the provinces and territories in Canada offer nonresident moose-hunting opportunities. Canada has the densest moose populations within all of North America by far. Moose hunting in any of the many different regions of Canada can include stalking through a wide variety of countless types of terrain, most of which are awe inspiring; others are jaw-droppingly beautiful and still others are astonishingly remote and inspiring. Just the scenery alone of each of the Canadian provinces and territories is worth the price of admission. Add that fact to the sheer concentration of moose throughout Canada and it becomes quickly obvious that a moose hunt in Canada is a moose hunt in the "promised land."

Most hunters who moose hunt in the United States either as residents or as nonresidents realize getting a moose license in the United States requires patience and time. It is not unusual for applicants to wait several years or more to draw a permit or to accumulate enough "preference points" to hunt moose in the few eastern and western states that actually offer moose hunting in the United States. (For seventeen years, I have applied to get a Maine nonresident moose license, and I haven't drawn one yet.)

Therefore, Canada is the most logical place in North America to plan a moose hunt because a majority of the provinces and territories do not have draws and preference points systems for nonresidents to be concerned about.

All the forthcoming moose-hunting information provided was current and pertinent as of this writing. However, moose-hunting regulations and dates in Canada (and the United States) can change from year to year and vary in each province and territory (and state). Therefore anyone hunting moose anywhere in Canada (or elsewhere) is strongly advised to research all such laws and regulations within the province or territory they plan to hunt *prior* to booking a hunt with a licensed Canadian guide or outfitter.

Canada consists of thirteen political divisions that include ten provinces and three territories. The provinces include from east to west:

- Newfoundland and Labrador
- Nova Scotia
- Prince Edward Island

- New Brunswick
- Quebec
- Ontario
- Manitoba
- Saskatchewan
- Alberta
- British Columbia

The major difference between a Canadian province and a Canadian territory is that a province is a creation of the Constitution Act (17 April 1982), while a territory is created by federal law. Thus, the federal government in Canada has more direct control over the territories, while provincial governments have many more competences and rights.

Eastern Canada (aka as the Eastern provinces) is generally considered to be the region of Canada east of Manitoba consisting of the following provinces:

- Newfoundland and Labrador
- New Brunswick
- Nova Scotia
- Ontario
- Prince Edward Island
- Quebec

Ontario and Quebec comprise the area known as Central Canada, while the other provinces constitute Atlantic Canada (the provinces of Nova Scotia, New Brunswick, and Prince Edward Island are also known as the Maritime Provinces).

The western provinces (east to west) include:

- Saskatchewan
- Alberta
- British Columbia

The three territories of Canada comprise the following:

- The Northwest Territory
- Nanuvat (the northernmost inhabited place in the world)
- Yukon

The moose densities in each province and territory as well as hunter success rates will vary throughout the country. When planning a moose hunt in Canada, do your homework regarding what province or territory you want to hunt by visiting either the tourism departments in each state and/or the game departments. Also be aware the cost of a Canadian moose hunt will differ considerably depending on where you hunt in Canada.

For instance, currently a prime destination for hunters seeking an opportunity to bag a world-class bull moose is in the Yukon Territory, where it is not uncommon to see bulls with antlers sixty inches in width or even exceeding seventy or more inches in width. A hunt here can cost as much as $16,000 to $20,000 dollars. A trophy-class bull-moose hunt in Newfoundland, where it is possible to take a mature bull with antlers ranging from forty-five inches wide to fifty inches wide and larger, will *generally* have a range of $4,500 to $5,500 in cost. So it is plain to see that prices vary considerably depending on where you hunt moose in Canada. A word of caution here: when it comes to hunting big game in Canada (or anywhere else for that matter), if the cost of the hunt is noticeably less than *most* other guides or outfitters are currently charging, a "RED FLAG" of caution should immediately go off in your mind. I can't tell you how many times I have heard absolute horror stories that revolved around "cheaper than normal" hunts.

The terrain and landscapes throughout Canada also differ extensively, and include a wide assortment of topography including mountainous regions, muskegs (western Canada), vast open bogs (elsewhere in Canada), swamps, ponds, lakes, heavily forested hardwoods, Tuckamore, and even some land that has views of or borders the Atlantic or Pacific Ocean coasts.

While Alaska certainly has excellent moose hunting, in my humble opinion, there is no better place in the world that offers more options to hunt moose than Canada.

NEWFOUNDLAND AND LABRADOR

The province of Newfoundland and Labrador is where my family and I do a majority of our moose hunting. The province comprises one of the last great wilderness areas in the world and I can *personally* attest to the fact that the province is an ultimate hunting destination—particularly for big game. Whether hunters want to set their sights on moose, rare woodland caribou, or black bear, or want to try for Newfoundland's revered "Newfoundland Grand Slam" of big-game hunting (taking all three big-game animals during one hunt), planning a big-game hunt in this amazing province is definitely the right choice.

Newfoundland has some of the most incredible pristine and challenging landscapes, abundant in trophy-sized big-game species, especially the Eastern moose.

Unlike other hunting destinations, in Newfoundland and Labrador you don't have to wait on a big-game license draw or be concerned about a lottery in order to obtain a license. A big-game license is included by the outfitter that you choose to book your hunt with. Speaking of Newfoundland outfitters, I have hunted in Newfoundland for moose (and caribou and bear) countless time during my fifty years of stalking big game worldwide.

I can say without a doubt through my years of experience hunting in Newfoundland, the guides and outfitters are among the most knowledgeable, experienced, hard-working, and friendly people I have hunted with worldwide. You can also count on them to know the land they hunt inside and out. Most of the outfitters' lodges are located within prime moose-hunting country. Moose-hunting adventures include everything from tent camps to deluxe lodges. Outfitters act as your main point of contact before and during your trip, so when booking a moose hunt in Newfoundland, be prepared to make long-lasting hunting memories and friends. As I often mention to big-game hunters I talk with about Newfoundland and Labrador, once you hunt moose or any other big game there, hunting in Newfoundland and Labrador becomes an addiction that is hard to break.

With some bulls weighing up to 1,200 pounds and carrying antlers that may have fifty-inch spreads, the total moose population on the islands is estimated at 120,000. Newfoundland has the most concentrated population in North America. Rifle hunters can hunt moose from September to December and regularly enjoy an established 85 percent success rate. And both bow and muzzleloader hunting is permitted in the province as well. Bow-hunting season opens earlier in August. Add to all of this an astounding *150,000 square miles of wilderness* and you can see how "your trigger finger should be getting itchy right about now."

Nonresident hunters are required to be accompanied by a licensed guide when they hunt big game. In fact, nonresident moose licenses are *only* available through a licensed outfitter in the province. This is actually the safest and most reliable way for nonresidents to realize the *most* success from their hunting adventure in Newfoundland and Labrador. You can visit www.nloa.ca for a detailed list of the province's professional guides and outfitters.

Michael Monaco with a dandy bull taken with NLOA member Newfoundland Big Game Adventures (www.nfbiggame.com).

NEWFOUNDLAND AND LABRADOR TOURISM

The Newfoundland and Labrador tourism website is a terrific source of information for all types of adventures in the province including hunting. You can visit their website at: www.Newfoundlandandandlabrador.com/hunting or call 800-563-6353 (Canada/US toll-free). The aforementioned website has a lot of trip planning information to share on the site as well. You'll find links to official websites of provincial and federal departments where you can obtain the latest detailed information on regulations covering big-game hunting, customs, passports, and firearms. For the latest hunting packages and trip planning information, sign up for their newsletter at www.NewfoundlandLabrador.com/enews. You will also discover some exciting hunting videos that you can view on their site as well.

NEWFOUNDLAND AND LABRADOR OUTFITTERS ASSOCIATION

An outfitter is the primary contact and source of information for any outdoor adventure in Newfoundland and Labrador. They will answer any and all of your questions regarding your trip or your hunting experience, and they welcome you to give them a call. An equally informative source for hunters planning a big-game adventure (or small game, fishing, etc.) can be found at the Newfoundland and Labrador Outfitters Association (NLOA) website at www.nloa.ca. It not only contains a list of the over 100 NLOA member outfitters, but it also provides a lot of other sources of outdoor adventure data as well. Be assured, by exploring the NLOA membership (I have included it below), you will locate the correct accommodations to suit your requirements and anticipations.

BOOKING A PACKAGE

Moose-hunting outfitter lodges and camps are located throughout the province in areas close to prime moose-hunting locations and populations. Big-game hunting licenses are obtained directly from the outfitter with whom a hunter books his trip, and the cost of the license can sometimes be included in the moose-hunting package price. Hunting quotas are set for each zone and are based on current population information and long-term management objectives.

I killed this bull after a long stalk at 235 yards using a Kimber .270WSM loaded with Winchester 150-grain Ballistic Silvertips. The massive bull died before he hit the ground. I was hunting with NLOA member Tuckamore Lodge (www.tuckamorelodge.com).

COMBO BIG-GAME PACKAGES

Many outfitters offer big-game combo packages that allow for clients to hunt woodland caribou and black bear. A hunter who stalks all three big-game species is hunting the province's legendary grand slam. Some outfitters also offer bow-hunting packages that include angling.

SEASON DATES

Season dates vary between Labrador and Newfoundland. Dates also vary from year to year by a few days. To find out specific dates for each species, visit: www. NewfoundlandLabrador.com/hunting.

HOW TO GET THERE

Air Canada (www.aircanada.com) is the primary carrier to Newfoundland. They can be reached by phone at 888-247-2262 (Canada/US toll-free). Air Canada's US partner is United Airlines (www.united.com).

To further share the amazing moose and other big-game hunting opportunities in this remarkable province of Newfoundland and Labrador, I have included below a few stories and pictures of our hunts and the animals we took.

THE BIG BULL INEXPLICABLY DISAPPEARED FROM OUR VIEW!

The helicopter lifted off the pad and headed toward our destination—a remote fly-in lodge called Arluk Tilt. In the native Inuit tongue, Arluk Tilt translates into "a place of comfort." Arluk Tilt would be our home away from home over the next week. Our hosts were Adrian Walsh and Alex Crosbie. Within minutes of liftoff we were flying over spectacular looking big-game backcountry. Thirty-five minutes later, the chopper descended to a lower altitude and angled sharply to the left as it cruised low over a salmon-choked river. I could feel the chopper slowing before I actually saw the lodge and within moments we were landing on a concrete pad in the middle of some of the most pristine wilderness I had ever seen.

It was just after noon by the time we unpacked our gear. Ada, the camp chef, a striking woman that has a host of outdoor skills including being a guide, made us a quick hot lunch. As soon as we finished eating, I sighted-in my firearm and Adrian suggested we use the remaining time in the day to go hunting. We packed our gear into the Argo and headed even further into the wilderness backcountry than we already were.

A little more than an hour later we were comfortably nestled in a group of rocks on a high peak overlooking a vast expanse of wilderness. As we sat and glassed, I barely felt the damp wind as it passed through my jacket without any effort. The anticipation of what was about to unfold kept my focus entirely riveted on a spot my guide, Randy, was glassing intensely. After several minutes, Randy spoke in a very hushed tone, even though the animal he was looking at was more than a mile away from us.

"I see a good bull moose in the valley below us," he whispered.

"Where is he?" I asked.

"He's tightly burrowed in an impenetrable cluster of Tuckamore trees." Tuckamore are the stunted balsam fir and spruce trees that grow in some alpine areas and along the coast. As we continued to glass the bull, Randy planned a stealth approach that would conceal us as we made our way down off the open ridge top. "We're going to have to move quickly and quietly if we're going to reach him without him detecting us. Once we get within 200 yards or so, I'll start calling and try to draw him out of the Tuckamore. Okay, let's get going," Randy whispered.

We used the natural cover of a deep draw to hide us for most of the way down the mountain and then carefully and slowly picked our way through a bog using any available cover we could to screen our final approach. We were closing in on the bull and were within 200 yards when we could hear and see him get up from his protected lair in the Tuckamore!

I have been hunting big game for more than fifty years, and hunting professionally as the host of the Woods N' Water Big Game Adventure TV series for the last thirty-two years. I have been both blessed and extremely fortunate to have been able to hunt a variety of big game throughout a majority of the states and provinces of North America and on the Dark Continent of Africa (along with my co-hosts, my wife, Kate, and my son Cody). I have stalked through the depths and deep gorge walls of the stunning Black Canyon in Colorado, tip-toed through the thickest patches of eerie black timber of Montana, hunted the haunting mountains of British Columbia in Canada, and chased game in deserts, canyon lands, glacier fields, swamps, mesquite-woods, farmlands, hardwoods, and every other type of memorable and scenic terrain imaginable. On one hunt, I was even lucky enough to have witnessed a rare migration of more than 10,000 barren-ground caribou as they migrated over the northern-most remote and picturesque landscapes in Kuujjuaq, Quebec, for days on end. All of these hunts have etched life-long experiences, images, and memories into my mind.

The one place I have no willpower to resist, and, therefore, I'm irresistibly drawn back to year after year, however, is by far the most alluring land I know—the Island Province of Newfoundland and Labrador. I assure you, this province is one of the last unspoiled wilderness areas in the world, and trust that Newfoundland and Labrador is the ultimate hunting destination, particularly when hunting big game. There is no shortage of pristine and challenging landscapes, and there is an abundance of trophy-sized big-game species. Unlike other hunting destinations, in Newfoundland and Labrador you don't have to wait on a big-game license draw or lottery for your license. Your big-game license is included in your hunting package purchased from the licensed outfitter.

Newfoundland and Labrador occupies a special place in my mind and heart—both of which harbor my most memorable and unforgettable outdoor experiences. But I digress—as the bull moose got up, we froze in place, in what seemed like a suspension of time. In reality, it was no more than seconds. We watched as the bull slowly swayed his antlers from side to side, as if he was struggling to locate a noise he heard. Then inexplicably, without any prior warning, he disappeared from our view. For a brief moment we were sure he had run off. Suddenly, Randy mouthed the words, "I hear him"! Then he whispered confidently, "Come on, I know where he's heading and we can get there before he does."

In one quick swoop the cameraman snatched up the camera and tripod, and in an instant we made a full-court press toward a small thicket of Tuckamore on a knob that overlooked a tiny open bog completely surrounded by a thick outcropping of balsam and spruce trees. Over the next hour we could hear the bull but couldn't see him. But Randy is a persistent guide and he continued to make several enticing cow calls, each one more seductive than the last. And still, the bull resisted his best efforts.

It was now late afternoon and time was beginning to go against us. To make matters worse, a heavy fog was slowly drifting off the surrounding mountains and heading toward us. Our only transportation was an Argo and we were at least one hour from the lodge. Things were getting dicey. If we overstayed our hunt, we were destined to spend an adventurous night in the field. Although the outfitter was prepared with enough gear including a tent, we all thought it was time to call off the hunt.

We had a quick powwow and Adrian and Randy said they felt we had about a half hour before we *had no choice* but to call the hunt off. Randy would make one last call and if the bull didn't respond, we agreed to head to camp immediately. Seconds after he ended his call, the form of the bull materialized from a group of thick balsam trees as if he were blown in there by a whiff of smoke. His body language made it crystal clear that he was hell-bent on making a direct line toward the direction of the last cow call. As soon as the bull stepped into the small opening, I placed the crosshairs of my scope on his front shoulder, eased the safety off, and steadily squeezed the trigger. At the report of the rifle shot, the 150-grain XP3 bullet smashed through the middle of the bull's front shoulder and he expired before he hit the ground. The bull had nineteen points and an inside spread of forty-five and a half inches, which is a real trophy-size moose in Newfoundland.

On his first trip to Newfoundland, my cousin and backup cameraman Ralph Somma took this terrific bull moose. It was taken on the same hunt described in this article. Unfortunately, I did not get a photo of my bull, but it was nearly identical, albeit slightly smaller, than Ralph's moose.

Because of our continuing concern about the incoming fog, two decisions had to be made. First, the bull had to be field dressed quickly, and second, it had to be retrieved by helicopter in the morning if we were to get back to the lodge before we were fogged in. We fired up the Argo and just over an hour later, with the fog now shrouding low over the entire countryside, we were waiting for dinner in the lodge while the ever-busy Randy stoked the woodstove. Over the next couple of days at Arluk Outfitters, my cameraman also bagged a dandy eighteen-point bull with a forty-five-inch spread and I took a good woodland caribou stag. It was a memorable and highly successful hunt that will be chalked up as one of the most enjoyable and adventuresome hunts I have been on.

If hunting for moose, woodland caribou, black bear, or any combination thereof is on your agenda, you should give the province of Newfoundland and Labrador serious consideration. It boasts, and rightfully so, of an incredible density of moose, a healthy woodland caribou herd and an abundance of big black bear. At Arluk Outfitters, Adrian told us that they regularly have a 100 percent success rate for woodland caribou and 90 or more percent on moose. Fall bear hunting is mostly a spot-and-stalk hunt and it, too, has a good success rate.

To get more information about Arluk Outfitters visit their website at www. arlukoutfitters.com. I promise you Arluk Outfitters will provide a quality hunt with a high success ratio and a terrific stay at either of their two lodges. Arluk doesn't take a lot of hunters per week. In fact, they like to book only two to three guests per week at their Arluk Tilt camp and, at their new lodge, no more than four hunters per week. These low guest numbers help to drastically cut the competition down each season, which helps tremendously to improve the hunting from year to year, which in turn increases their overall guest success-rate ratio considerably.

If you are interested in watching the entire television show we produced about our big-game hunt at Arluk Outfitters, you can see the program on YouTube. Once there, enter "Peter Fiduccia Woods N' Water" and click on "Arluk Outfitters" to watch all three big-game hunts.

Despite all attempts by "Murphy's Law" to ruin my son's hunt by a comedy of errors caused by me, Lady Luck finally intervened. After Cody's guide, Tim, called the bull in for a third time, Cody got a broadside shot that sent the bull sliding nose down into the bog. The bull was taken at Island Safaris (www.islandsafaris.com).

A FATHER-SON MOOSE HUNT TO REMEMBER

Sometimes Murphy's Law enjoys throwing a couple of curve balls into the spokes of a well-running wheel during a big-game adventure. That turned out to be the case during my son's (P. Cody's) first ever moose hunt. To make a long story short, due to a variety of bad luck, bad timing, and an intense three-day rain storm, Cody didn't get end up taking a bull on the hunt. While the guide, Cody, and Kate (who was the cameraperson on the hunt) worked hard climbing mountains, crossing never ending bogs, and glassing the terrain for hours each day, they never got close enough to a good bull to "close the deal." Although Cody took it in stride and enjoyed all the adventure, scenery, and anticipation that are part and parcel of any hunt, being a father, I couldn't help feel disappointed for him. So I secretly planned another moose hunt for him for the following fall.

On the morning of his second moose hunt at Island Safaris (www.islandsafaris.com), "Murphy" once again tried to deal Cody a bad hand. It all began when I got up extra early to shower before leaving for a day of hunting. While turning to get the shampoo, I severely wrenched my back out of place. It hurt so bad I couldn't straighten up for a few hours. Around 10 a.m. I glanced over at Cody who looked both worried for me and anxious that we might miss the first day of his hunt. At that moment I knew I had to suck it up, and I decided to take a 500 milligram pain killer (Percocet, which was prescribed for me after a knee surgery) to help lessen the pain. Within an hour, the pain was masked enough for me to put on a good "game face." So I said to our guide, Tim Sheppard, and Cody, "Hey fellas, I'm feeling much better. Let's go hunting!"

By noon our guide Tim, Cody, and I were glassing a ridge top about two miles away. About an hour later the guide spotted a good bull sky-lined at the top of the ridge. He turned to me and said, "I know this bull is heading to a clearing at the end of this trial to look for cows in a nearby bog. If we move quickly we may be able to cut him off as he crosses through the clearing. Peter, is your back good enough to get down the trail in a hurry?"

Out of the corner of my eye I could see the high anticipation in Cody's face as he waited to hear my response. "Tim, I'm fine—lead the way!" While pain shot through my back with each step, I put it out of my mind. About twenty-five minutes later, we reached the trail's end. Cody and I sat at the edge of a bunch of Tuckamore trees at the very end of what was now a very visible trail.

Tim walked about fifty yards from Cody and me and began making a series of enticing cow calls. It wasn't long before we could hear the sounds of a bull approaching, grunting and bellowing deeply as he got closer. Within minutes he was directly below us, walking through a tangle of thick pines and blow downs. We could see bits and pieces of him as he made his way up the embankment, and he appeared to be moving steadily to where the trail ended. As Tim had so accurately predicted, the bull was heading directly toward the small clearing. I pressed the "record" button on the camera, began rolling tape, and gave Cody the signal that I was ready.

For whatever reason the bull suddenly stopped in his tracks and, in one fluid motion turned, and trotted back the way he came! We were all stunned and disappointed. Tim quickly walked over to us and put his finger to his lips, motioning to us to be quiet. Then, without even whispering a word, he gave us a hand signal to follow him.

We hurriedly made our down the embankment toward a creek far below. Tim and Cody were moving so quickly, I was getting nauseous and light-headed from the motion, which I suspected was caused by the pain medication. Suddenly Tim stopped, yanked a piece of plywood that looked like a moose antler out of his backpack, and started frantically raking a tree while making grunt vocalizations. I had barely gotten the camera on the tripod and started rolling tape when the bull dashed from the bush and headed right toward us.

The excitement didn't help my condition, and I could feel the blood rushing to my head. Although I was desperately trying to get the bull in focus, I simply couldn't see him well enough in the viewfinder to do so, even though he was standing perfectly still and staring at us only fifty yards away. I was getting very dizzy with each passing moment, and when I turned to signal Cody to shoot, I bumped the tripod and camera. That was all it took for the bull to instantly turn himself inside out—and he was gone in a blink of an eye.

It is hard to put in words how badly I felt, or how dejected tim was, or the look on my son's face. I was about to apologize when Tim again motioned to us to be quiet and follow him. Cody hesitated and whispered, "Dad, I don't want to go after this bull. I'm really worried about you." I smiled at him and said, "I'm sorry for messing that up. It's the medication, nothing more. Don't worry, let's go."

When we caught up with Tim a minute later, he was raking a tree, trashing brush, and making grunts. Cody's quickly set up his rifle on his shooting sticks and steadied himself. We could hear the bull in the bush but couldn't see him. Then, like a whiff of smoke, he emerged from a thick grove of Tuckamore swinging his head in an exaggerated side-to-side motion and grunting. With the camera rolling and the bull in focus, I whispered, "I've got him. Take him, son!"

Almost instantaneously after my remark, I heard the report of Cody's .300WSM echo across the valley. The 180-grain XP3 smacked the bull hard, squarely in the shoulder. Through the viewfinder I could see every muscle on the bull momentarily flinch tightly. Then the bull turned, ran about twenty-five yards, and then plummeted to the ground, his nose plowing up forest debris like a snowblade plows away snow.

Cody anxiously looked at me and asked, "Dad, did you get it all on tape?"

"I think I did," I replied.

Although I had seen everything in the viewfinder of the camera, at that moment, I was not sure if I had videotaped the bull or not. I was so dizzy from the medication at this point, I wasn't even sure I pressed the record button!

As it turned out, the entire hunt and all three encounters with the bull were on tape. The day ended spectacularly well despite "Murphy's" attempt to ruin it.

My son took his first bull moose, a terrific sixteen-pointer, with one clean shot. I was filled with excitement and pride for Cody. By time we field-dressed the bull it was pitch-dark, and the three of us slowly picked our way along the old worn-out logging trail back to where we had left the truck.

For the first hundred yards or so not a word was spoken by anyone. Then Cody stopped in his tracks, turned to me, and said, "Thanks dad, I know you were really hurting and I appreciate what you did for me today." Then he smiled and hugged me—for a long time.

Cody is an accomplished vocalist who studied opera at the Manhattan School of Music. However, for whatever reason, he rarely sings in front of me. As we continued down the logging trail, he began signing, in an animated manner, two of my most favorite songs—"Brother Can You Spare a Dime" and "Fly Me to the Moon." I suspect it was his way of showing me how ecstatic he actually was. It was a fitting way to end the first day of our father-son hunt.

For the record, I was supposed to hunt after Cody took his bull. Over the next several hours the pain became so intolerable I had to leave the lodge. The next day I went to the airport, purchased two tickets, and flew home. After seeing my doctor I spent several days in bed and several more days in therapy recovering. But I assure you, I'd do it all over again, because the memory of that hunt will last with both Cody and me for a lifetime, and cherished memories are something Newfoundland is renowned for providing to big-game hunters.

Cody poses with his terrific sixteen-point bull taken with NLOA member outfitter Island Safaris.

A REMOTE FLY-IN BULL FOR KATE

The helicopter flew what seemed like a dart-like straight line for nearly forty-five minutes over a variety of gorgeous Newfoundland scenery. We were on our way to one of Grey River Lodges' (www.greyltd.com) remote camps called Caribou. My wife, Kate, was going to hunt for her Canadian moose. Several years earlier, Kate had drawn a once-in-a-lifetime moose license in Utah where she took a small Shiras bull during heavy snowfall that tuned into a blizzard. On this trip she was hoping for better weather and a chance to bag a respectable Eastern Canadian moose in the province of Newfoundland and Labrador.

As the chopper banked sharply to the right and dropped altitude, we watched as the lodge below quickly rose up to greet us. Our outfitter, Tony Tuck, was waving and smiling as the helicopter gently touched down on the landing pad. Camp Caribou looked like it was going to be "home" for Kate and I over the next several days.

The first day of the hunt a friend of ours, Markus Wilhelm, took a good bull. We watched his entire hunt unfold from nearly a mile away as we sat near a large rock across a lake (lakes are referred to as "ponds" by the locals). The next two days were spent indoors as a hurricane moved through the province.

On the fourth day of our hunt, the weather cleared and we were boating along the shoreline when our host and guide, Tony Tuck, saw a bull with some cows up high on the mountainside slowly crisscrossing the landscape that bordered the east side of the "pond." From what we could see of the bull, he looked like a "keeper."

Tony thought the best course of action was to get on shore and glass the bull and cows in order to get an idea of what they were going to do next. This way, we could formulate a good stalk. At one point the moose disappeared into the bush for more than an hour or so. We were about to start up the mountainside when Tony spotted them again.

He thought if we could make a wide circle and get above them we might have a good chance of calling the bull in. As we discussed our strategy, we saw the moose bed down in some low Tuckamore. Tony built a fire and while we watched them we ate lunch and drank some hot tea.

Then Tony said, "Come on, let's go get that bull," and we began the arduous steep climb up the mountainside. Every couple of hundred yards or so Tony would stop, and we would glass the moose to make sure they were still bedded where we had last seen them.

About two hours later we reached an area that Tony thought was about 200 yards above where the moose were bedded down. He told Kate to load her rifle and get it set up on her shooting sticks, then he told me to get the camera setup on the tripod—which it already was!

We waited about thirty minutes, and then Tony began to make several love-sick cow calls. Although I don't think any of us expected it, the bull answered Tony's calls immediately. We could see him looking up toward were we were in a vain attempt to find what he thought was a cow in estrus.

Tony turned to Kate and whispered, "I don't think we can stop this guy from coming; he's heading our way fast, be ready." Over the next fifteen minutes, I could sense Kate's anticipation and anxiety levels elevating. With each call Tony made, the bull brazenly replied and continued to move closer to us.

Then Tony made a bull call and I could see the bull's demeanor instantly change. He pinned his ears back and, with his cows, started trotting toward us. I could hear Tony whisper to Kate, "They're going to pass by us along that trail just above us—are you ready?" I saw Kate nod yes and heard the safety flip off on her rifle.

Then the first cow trotted by, followed by a couple of calves and the bull. By now the whites of his eyes were glaring and he looked like he was spoiling for a fight with the anticipated but imaginary competitor he heard. The bull was less than fifty yards above us, grunting as he moved along.

As he passed us he caught sight of the camera on the tripod and turned his neck quickly and sharply toward it. That's when I barely heard Kate whisper, "I'm taking him." The shot from her .308 Kimber echoed through the valley below us. The bull's shoulder took the full impact of the 150-grain Winchester Ballistic Silvertip bullet, and he was finished before he ever hit the ground!

Kate's dandy bull—her first Eastern Canadian moose. Kate also bagged bulls in Utah and other areas of Newfoundland. The hunt was with NLOA member outfitter Grey River Lodge (www.greyltd.com).

The celebration was joyous, and Kate was elated to have the opportunity to take good bull as well as enjoy a fantastic stalk and one-shot kill. You can see that hunt on the Grey River website at www.greyltd.com, titled "Woods N' Water TV Show" or on YouTube under "Peter Fiduccia's Woods N' Water."

LATE-SEASON MOOSE HUNTING

One last thought about hunting moose in Newfoundland—hunters don't always have to book their hunt during the rut to be successful. Actually, during the late season, which is considered to be November and December, hunters will have what many outfitters believe to be "an equally good or better chance to see and bag a mature bull."

During the late season bulls begin to ban together in areas to feed and seek shelter. It isn't unusual for a hunter to see half dozen bulls or more during a day of scouting, glassing, and hunting. During the 2013 season I went on a moose hunt with Red Indian Lake Outfitting and Tours (www.redindianlake.com).

When I arrived the snow was well over a foot deep, the temperatures were well below freezing, and the wind was blowing hard. On the first morning of our hunt the weather went from bad to worse. Despite that, we glassed over a dozen bulls during the day along with twice that amount of cows.

The next day it was cold but sunny. It had rained hard all night and a lot of the snow had melted. Again, we saw a lot of bulls during our day afield. In fact, on that day we stalked two different bulls. The first was with a group of three bulls that all had decent sets of antlers. We glassed the bulls from a high point about a mile or so away, which is the way most moose hunting is done in Newfoundland, and then my guide Fred laid out a plan of attack. We descended the mountain as quickly as the calf-high snow and my bad knee would allow. When we got to the bottom we jumped in the Argo and closed the distance to about 500 yards. It took nearly an hour to slowly approach along an old logging road to reach the bulls who were feeding in a tiny clearing.

When we got to the spot, we discovered we had to climb up off the road onto a steep bank in order to see the threesome. Unfortunately, our stalk ended with only Fred getting to see the bulls. As I approached with my cameraman, the moose heard our approach and were gone in an instant.

Undeterred, the ever-optimistic Fred went back to the high point and began glassing again. Literally minutes later as I was talking on camera to update the audience on our hunt, Fred spotted a "big bull that had a large set of antlers." With a quick game plan, Fred, another of his guides, my cameraman, and I got in the Argo and headed toward the area where the bull was.

Once there we hiked up a steep mountain and stalked along the ridge until we could see the three bulls and several cows feeding in the open below us. I quickly set up my rifle on the tripod. Fred pointed and I placed my crosshairs on the shoulder of the largest antlered bull that was about 175 yards below me. The first shot smacked the bull squarely in the shoulder, but instead of crumbling to the ground the bull ran off and Fred stopped him by making a cow call.

A note of interest here about late-season moose hunts. I've been on three over the year and I can tell you, as many guides in Newfoundland will as well, a bull will still respond to a cow call after the rut. I have seen bulls called in from very late October through the end of the season in late December. It is, and I assure you of this, not unusual for a Newfoundland guide (or I'm sure guides from other provinces) to call in moose well after the prime rut is over. Therein lies the key to hunting moose in the late season: not only do hunters get to see many more bulls during that time of year, they can enjoy the excitement and thrill of having a guide call one in for them as well.

Getting back to my bull, after he stopped, I squeezed off a second shot and he dropped in his tracks. My late-season moose hunt ended with a dandy eighteen-point bull taken when hunting seems like it was meant to happen, during a time of year when snowflakes fly and cold weather exhilarates.

I strongly urge any moose hunter to consider a late-season moose hunt in Newfoundland or anywhere. A late-season hunt will provide a terrific opportunity to bag a bull of a lifetime as well as a hunt to remember for many years to come.

This bull was spotted eating with three other bulls and several cows by my guide, Fred Thorne, from one of Fred's favorite lookout points. Late-season hunts can often produce more sightings of bull moose per day than when hunting during the rut. Bulls can still be called in during the late season as well: Fred used a cow call to entice the bull closer. I took the bull in December at Red Indian Lake Outfitting & Tours (www.redindianlake.com).

NOVA SCOTIA

There are no moose-hunting licenses available to nonresidents in the province of Nova Scotia.

However, Nova Scotia residents that want to hunt moose in Nova Scotia are currently restricted to Inverness and Victoria Counties of Cape Breton Island. Licenses are issued through a lottery-draw process. The application period occurs annually, each spring. More information is available online at www.novascotia.ca/natr/draws/moosedraw.

PRINCE EDWARD ISLAND

While Prince Edward Island is remarkably beautiful and offers excellent fishing and other tourism opportunities, there are no moose on the island and therefore no moose hunting is available. You can visit this website to discover all other types of outdoor and other activities: www.tourismpei.com.

NEW BRUNSWICK

Both residents and nonresidents of New Brunswick who want to hunt moose must enter the appropriate annual draw process. Nonresident applicants must be at least eighteen years of age at the time of application, and they must not be restricted from purchasing a New Brunswick hunting license.

Resident moose draw applicants must have New Brunswick as their principal place of residence, be the holder of a valid New Brunswick Medicare Card, and be at least eighteen years of age at the time of application. They must not be restricted from purchasing a New Brunswick hunting license. Exceptions: Royal Canadian Mounted Police and DND personnel may apply by using their identification card number.

The allocations for resident moose-hunting licenses are determined on an annual basis for each of New Brunswick's wildlife management zones. Resident draw applicants must choose their zone at the time of application. Nonresident hunters may choose their zone at the time they pick up their hunting license.

Anyone interested in information about resident or nonresident moose draws may do so by contacting the offices of the Department of Natural Resources and Service New Brunswick centers or on the Department of Natural Resources website: www2.gnb.ca/content/gnb/en/departments/natural_resources.html.

To make it more convienient, New Brunswick allows applications to be applied for by telephone or on the Department of Natural Resources website.

In 2014, moose-hunting season dates are from the twenty-fifth to the twenty-seventh of September. Nonresidents can apply online from February 10 to the April 30. Results are made available from May 12 to June 13. Check with the New Brunswick DNR for accurate dates of subsequent seasons and license sales. To locate a guide, browse the New Brunswick Professional Outfitter Guide Association at www.nepoga.com.

New Brunswick general information:
Telephone: (506) 453-3826
Reception: (506) 453-3826
Fax: (506) 444-4367
Email: dnr_mrnweb@gnb.ca
Website: www.gnb.ca/naturalresources
Mailing Address:
Hugh John Flemming Forestry Centre
P. O. Box 6000
Fredericton, NB
E3B 5H1
Canada

QUEBEC

At this writing, nonresident moose licenses are only valid in the zone(s) that are listed on the hunter's license. Hunting moose in any other zone or zones is strictly prohibited. Nonresidents who wish to hunt for *cow* moose must register to apply for a special random-draw permit. Before a nonresident plans to hunt for moose in Quebec, it is particularly wise to check out all moose-hunting regulations thoroughly prior to applying for a moose license. The laws change regularly, sometimes from year to year. The best up-to-date information can be found at www.mddep.gouv.qc.ca. A list of Quebec's guides can be found at www.outfittersand-guides.com/quebec.

ONTARIO

The province of Ontario is proud of its long-standing hunting tradition and of its solid reputation for delivering all the beauty and adventure of the great outdoors and all the opportunities for a safe and successful hunt. In Ontario, "moose are emblems of the outdoors, the royalty of the wilderness." Moose populations are controlled through strict, selective harvest programs that *limit* the taking of animals with high reproductive potential. According to the Ontario game department, the result of this practice has provided a plentiful population of moose in the allowable hunting areas that is estimated to be at about 99,000 animals. There are estimated an additional 15,000 moose that roam within the remote and protected areas of Ontario.

Moose hunting in Ontario is both challenging and rewarding. Tactics range from calling and lying in wait in cutovers, new burns, marsh meadows, bogs, and lake narrows to tracking moose along game trails. No matter what method or tactic a hunter prefers, Ontario outfitters offer myriad opportunities to experience "the rush of the chase."

Nonresident moose-hunting areas offer gun seasons (rifle, shotgun, and muzzleloader) and a bow-only seasons from September to mid-November. An adult cow in Ontario can weigh as much as 800 pounds and an Ontario bull in his prime can tip the scales at an unbelievable 1,400 pounds.

Nonresident hunters who want to plan a moose hunt in Ontario must have valid hunting accreditation from another state or province and be "registered as a guest and accommodated by an outfitter authorized to issue nonresident moose validations tags." The outfitters within Ontario offer a wide range of options, from drive-to camps with all the amenities to remote fly-in outposts miles from the nearest beaten path or road. Hunting lodges are important for nonresident moose hunters. To locate an outfitter in Ontario go to www.ontariooutfittersnetwork.com.

Use the following resources to learn more about hunting and licenses in Ontario and the regulations that you will be required to follow. The Ministry of Natural Resources (MNR) is concerned with the protection of the province's environment and wildlife. Their website outlines all the provincial regulations pertaining to hunting and fishing, as well as updates and articles of note. You can visit the MNR website at www.mnr.gov.on.ca.

For a full, up-to-date listing of general hunting information—including important dates and phone numbers, general regulations, moose regulations, hunter safety, definitions, license information, Wildlife Management Unit maps, important messages for hunters, and a lot more—go to www.mnr.gov.on.ca.

All the information you need to know about the rules, regulations, and procedures regarding firearms and ammunition can be located at the website of the Canadian Firearms Center at www.cfc-cafa.gc.ca.

Moose hunting begins mid-September and continues through mid-December. When hunting from the middle of November into December, expect to see snow on the ground. Snow will make hunting and tracking a trophy moose a lot easier in Northern Ontario's Algoma area! Like other outfitters within this province, Algoma's professionals will cater to you for accommodations, meals, guide services, trophy mounting, and the packing and shipping of your game to your requested destination point.

MANITOBA

Manitoba offers exciting opportunities for hunting a variety of big-game animals. Nonresidents can hunt for moose (in some areas). Moose-hunting seasons (as with caribou and elk) are based on a Game Hunting Area (GHA) system. Licenses are only valid in the GHA or GHAs specified for that season. Black bear, gray wolf, and white-tailed deer seasons are based on a grouping of GHAs as zones. Licenses are valid in all zones, but season dates vary by zone.

To hunt big-game moose and other big game in Manitoba, all foreign-resident hunters must book their hunt through a *registered* lodge or outfitter. The outfitter or guide must be authorized to "outfit foreign resident hunters." It is also mandatory for all foreign-resident hunters to be accompanied by a licensed Manitoba guide at all times while in the field, with no more than three hunters per guide. Nonresident hunters must only use the services of the outfitter specified on their hunting license.

When bringing firearms into Manitoba (or anywhere else in Canada), foreign-resident hunters are advised to contact the Canadian Firearms Center for information on permits, cost, possession, storage, and transportation. More information can be found at www.rcmp-grc.gc.ca. Also, it is recommended that foreign-resident hunters contact the Canada Border Services Agency when crossing the border from United States into Manitoba: www.cbsa-asfc.gc.ca.

Nonresidents shipping or transporting big game out of the province or the country may be required to meet certain conditions and/or obtain relevant permits.

Be sure to review the appropriate section in the hunting regulations guide for more information on the species you wish to hunt. Copies of this guide are available at any Manitoba Conservation and Water Stewardship Office, at www.gov. mb.ca, and at hunting-license vendors. The easiest way to locate a guide or outfitter in the province of Manitoba is to visit www.mloa.com.

SASKATCHEWAN

Saskatchewan is one of Canada's great "Prairie Provinces." Saskatchewan lies west of Manitoba, east of Alberta, north of North Dakota and Montana, and south of the Northwest Territory. The province covers a total area of over 250,000 square miles, over 13,000 square miles of which are inland water. Texas is the only US state larger than Saskatchewan.

Saskatchewan offers surprisingly good moose-hunting opportunities. Just recently the province raised its moose-hunting limits due to more fatal car crashes involving moose. Saskatchewan's moose populations have grown significantly over the past decade. Moose sightings used to be much less common in the southern part of the province, but now 10 percent of the Saskatchewan's estimated 50,000 moose live in southern regions of the province.

Nonresident hunters will find new opportunities to stalk farmland moose. Moose populations throughout the farmlands of Saskatchewan continue to increase. Therefore, quotas increased by 875 licenses in 2013 and may increase again.

The province is also opening new zones. For the first time, either-sex moose-hunting opportunities will be offered in several zones including 2, 5, 15, 16, 51, 52, and Buckland-Prince Albert Wildlife Management Zone. There will be new antlerless moose quotas in Zones 6A, 8A/11A, 36A, and 40A. Quotas in the remaining farmland zones have been adjusted to balance population levels with occurrences of moose/human interactions. For information on the current and new zones, licenses, game laws, and more visit www.tourismsaskatchewan.com. You can also go to www.enviroment.gov.sk.ca or www.huntingtripsrus.com. A list of guides belonging to The Saskatchewan Outfitters Association can be found at www.soa.com.

ALBERTA

Alberta consists of five areas, including Northern Boreal 500 Series and 841, Foothills 300 Series, Parkland 200 Series, 728, 730, and 936, Prairie 100 Series, and Mountain 400 Series.

Alberta moose-hunting outfitters have taken moose that range in body weights of 1,500 pounds or more! Antlers can range from generally forty-five to fifty inches in width to mature bulls having antlers that are in the sixty-inch class. Alberta's moose management is designed to ensure moose are not overharvested, which allows hunters to enjoy both quantity and quality moose-hunting opportunities in Alberta. One of the more famous areas for quality moose is the Peace River country in northwestern Alberta. It is a prime moose habitat area producing trophy-class antlers. Moose hunting is generally very good throughout Alberta and the province can offer opportunities for some trophy-class animals.

While moose hunting in Alberta starts in late August, most moose hunting occurs from mid-September through early October during the peak time of the rut. During this time, calling and raking are the standard hunting methods. In some zones moose can be hunted as late as December. During this timeframe the rut is over and the primary tactic in Alberta is spot and stalk. Hunters can harvest trophy-class bulls during this time of the year as they are more mobile and predictable.

Whether you hunt Alberta's golden plains, parklands, boreal forests, or alpine peaks and valleys, the territories are as diverse as its wildlife. Big-game hunters come to Alberta in droves during the autumn for a chance at bagging elk, cougar, antelope, whitetail or mule deer, bighorn sheep, bear, and particularly moose.

As with planning a hunt anywhere, make the most of your hunting experience by doing your homework and research long before booking your hunt. In Alberta, nonresident hunters are required to use the services of a professional hunting guide. There are many outfitters who specialize in moose hunting. Visit Alberta Professional Outfitters Society at www.apos.ar.com for a complete list of all licensed and registered guides in Alberta.

There are many game laws nonresident hunters should familiarize themselves with including license and permit regulations as well as general hunting game laws which can be found at www.albertaregulations.ca. To get information on licenses and permits, a good source is www.mywildalberta.com.

BRITISH COLUMBIA

The big-game hunting choices are endless in British Columbia, and they are all set in spectacular natural settings. Adult bulls in British Columbia reach sizes that exceed six feet in height at the shoulder and have some of the largest antlers and body weights of moose found in North America. British Columbia has three subspecies of moose. While all three subspecies are similar in appearance, the moose found in southeastern British Columbia have the smallest bodies and antlers. The biggest moose are found in northern British Columbia.

The moose here look noticeably different from other native moose in the province, and they are one of the most widely distributed ungulates in British Columbia. Found across almost the entire interior of the province, they are most abundant in the central and sub-boreal interior, the northern boreal mountains, and the boreal plains of northeastern British Columbia. With the exception of a few dry mountainous areas within the province, moose are also common in most of the mountainous valleys.

Moose survive in these areas by moving along the rivers that cut through the Coast Range and by foraging in dense browse stands that occur at or near the estuaries of those rivers. According to the latest figures provided, British Columbia has about 170,000 moose. Over 70 percent live in northern British Columbia and the rest in the Cariboo-Chilcotin, Thompson-Okanagan, and Kootenay regions.

Population densities of moose in the province vary greatly from place to place, due mostly to snow depth and the availability of winter browse. During winter, typical population densities in British Columbia range from one-third moose per mile to about one and a half per mile.

Over the last few decades, moose have been one of the most important game species in British Columbia, providing more meat than all other deer (ungulates) combined. The moose is also a valued trophy animal and the number of animals harvested within the province is about 8,000 to 14,000 animals per year. Moose hunting has generated considerable license revenue for management, habitat enhancement, and enforcement programs, as well as income for guides, outfitters, and their assistants in British Columbia's northern communities.

All nonresident big-game hunters in the province of British Columbia must be accompanied by a registered guide and outfitter *or* accompanied by a resident who holds a "Permit to Accompany." Visit www.outfitterpros.com for a complete list of registered professional guides in the province. Once you have booked a guide or an "accompany hunter" that has received his/her PTA paperwork you may purchase a hunting license through the mail. You must fill out the Nonresident Hunting License Application available at www.env.gov.bc.ca and mail it to the Fish and Wildlife Branch along with your payment. If you decide to purchase your own license, definitely let your guide or permit holder know that you are doing so. Generally, guides and permit holders will often purchase licenses for hunters. To avoid the possibility of applying and receiving two licenses communicate with your guide and decide who will be getting the license. It is not legal and it is an offense for nonresidents to have more than one hunting license. For more detailed, up-to-date nonresident moose-hunting information on license fees, season dates, laws, hunter education requirements, zones, maps, and much more, visit the Ministry of Forests, Lands, and Natural Resource Operations at www.envgov. bc.ca./fw/wildlife/hunting/regulations.

For more detailed information on hunting moose in British Columbia you can contact the Fish and Wildlife Branch Ministry of Environment to talk with them regarding your questions.

PO Box 9374

Stn Prov Govt, Victoria, BC

V8W 9M4

Canada

Telephone: Toll free 1-800-663-7867 or local 250 356-1427

Fax: 250 387-0239

You can also contact Fish, Wildlife Branch by mail:
PO Box 939
Stn Prov Govt, Victoria, BC
V8W 9M8
Canada
Telephone: 250-387-9771
For limited entry inquires *only*, call 250-356-5142.

THE NORTHWEST TERRITORY

There are eight regions within the Northwest Territories (NWT). They include the Western Arctic, Mackenzie Heartland, Dehcho, Nahanni Country, Northern Frontier, Yellowknife, Great Slave Gateway, and Wood Buffalo. Although NWT are known mostly for the spectacular autumn and winter midnight natural show known as the Northern Lights, the NWT are also home to some of the finest moose hunting found in the world.

The NWT is home to a wide range of wildlife including moose, caribou, muskox, bison, wolves, and polar, grizzly, and black bears, and Dall's sheep. Big bulls are commonplace in the NWT and many of them exceed weights of 1,500 pounds and have antlers that regularly exceed sixty or sixty-five inches in width, and some carry antlers wider than that.

Moose are widely found throughout the NWT. They are generally found in areas with semi-open forest cover that have an abundance of willow and aspen stands and are close to lakes, rivers, stream banks, sandbars, and valleys.

Moose are managed by controlling the hunting season for resident and nonresident hunters. While residents of the NWT can hunt moose from September 1 to January 31, nonresident seasonal hunters "are only allowed" to hunt moose between September 1 and October 31.

Nonresidents require a license to hunt in the NWT and all hunting regulations are determined by the Department of Environment and Natural Resources. It is not uncommon for the Renewable Resource Officers (RRO) to routinely inspect hunters at checkpoints, at border crossings, and in hunting areas to check they are in compliance with all NWT hunting regulations. Therefore it is highly suggested that hunters familiarize themselves with the laws regarding the game they are hunting.

Hunting rights of the Aboriginal people in the NWT are founded on "traditional use" and they can be unlike the hunting rights and/or laws of other hunters. Hunting by others may also be different and therefore affected by Land Claim Agreements with the Aboriginal peoples. An interesting note is that the Tlicho people call moose "Dendi," the Gwich'in call them "Dinjik," and they are called "Æîts'é" in North Slavey language.

In the NWT all hunters are required to have a valid hunting license (wildlife tag) to hunt for moose and other big game that is not being hunted for "food." Nonresidents, Canadian citizens, or landed immigrants who live outside the NWT, and nonresident aliens—people who live outside of the NWT and Canada—must have an outfitter to hunt big game. Outfitters provide licensed guides for their hunting clients. Wildlife tags are issued for each species. Tags are part of the hunting license and must be attached to the animal "*immediately*" after it is killed. Like many other provinces and territories in Canada, licenses and tags must be carried on your person while hunting. Licenses must be signed to be valid and they are not transferable.

Nonresident big-game licenses and tags may *only* be purchased at Environment and Natural Resources (ENR) offices: www.enr.gov.nt.ca.

Information regarding outfitters of the NWT can be obtained from the NWT Tourism Association at www.spectacularnwt.com.

NUNAVUT (THE NORTHERNMOST INHABITED PLACE IN THE WORLD)

Big-game hunting is a part of Nunavut's tourism industry, for good reason. While Nunavut doesn't offer moose hunting for either residents or nonresidents, it does feature some of the most *exotic* and highly prized big-game animals on Earth, including "extremely dangerous polar bears," numerous herds of muskox, plentiful barren-ground caribou, a sustainable harvest of walrus, and the healthiest and least threatened population of wolves in the world. More interestingly, while researching this information, I spoke with Arron Watson, manager of the Unikkaarvik Visitor Center. Arron told me that the rare barren-ground grizzly bear, which is a cross between a polar bear and a grizzly bear, are seen in western Hudson Bay in the Kivalliq region. Aaron also mentioned that while there is *no moose hunting* in Nanuvut, there have been "recent sightings" of moose mostly around the "southern edges of Nanuvut. For additional big-game information in Nanuvut, visit www.nanuvuttourism.com. You can also visit the Unikkaarvik Visitor Center website at www.nunavuttourism.com, or contact them toll free from North America: 1-866-686-2888.

YUKON TERRITORY

The Yukon Territory is highly well known for its wild and uncompromising land, home to a wide variety of big-game species. The terrain includes mountains, high plateaus, grassy slopes, and deer-forested valleys and ravines, all containing a diverse habitat for all of the Yukon's big-game animals. Over 40 percent of the Yukon is covered in boreal forests, and about 80 percent of the Yukon is classified as "wilderness." That accounts for the animals being less pressured than in other hunting states and provinces.

The Yukon is the "Mecca" of moose hunting in Canada. There are about 70,000 moose in the Yukon, and according to biologists, the Yukon moose population is said to be stable and steadily "growing." Two of the four recognized subspecies of moose found worldwide reside in the Yukon. The largest subspecies, the Yukon-Alaska moose (*Alces alces gigas*) are found in the northern portion of the territory. The Canadian moose (*Alces alces andersoni*) is found in the southern portions of the territory. There is no precise boundary between these two subspecies.

It is said that some Yukon moose can reach a height of seven feet at their shoulder and reach unimaginable weights of 1,800 pounds! Yukon moose are said to be at least "20 percent bigger" than the Eastern Moose found in eastern Canada and northeast United States. The average antler spread of an Alaska-Yukon moose is generally fifty-five to sixty inches wide. However, a mature Yukon bull-moose can measure over six feet (and seventy-two inches in antler width), with the highest record set of trophy antlers reaching an astonishing eighty-four inches in width. That kind of potential width is what makes moose hunters dream of booking a hunt in the Yukon.

The general consensus from dozens of folks I have talked with about their moose-hunting excursions in the Yukon was "It's incredible." Most outfitters report a 100 percent success rate and the balance claim of success rates ranging from 90 to 100 percent.

A nonresident who wants to hunt moose in the Yukon must be guided by a registered Yukon outfitter. You can research Yukon's registered guides at www. yukonoutfitters.net. Nonresident Canadians must also be guided by a registered Yukon outfitter *or* guided by a Yukon resident holding a special guide license. To demonstrate how popular nonresident moose hunting is: at the time of this writing (May 2014), all 2014–15 special guide licenses were sold out by April of this year.

Under a special guide license, only specific species may be hunted and only in specific areas; moose, caribou, wolf, coyote, black bear, and grizzly bear can all be hunted under a special guide license. Bison, goat, sheep, elk, and wolverine may not. It is important to note that when a nonresident hunts in the Yukon, he or she must pay "harvest fees on any big game animals killed," prior to leaving the Yukon.

To find out more detailed information on hunting in the Yukon visit The Department of Tourism and Culture of the Government of Yukon at www.tc.gov.yk.ca.

13 CLOTHING

During moose seasons across North America, temperatures will vary greatly day to day. From Maine to Newfoundland, you could encounter snowfall one day and seventy-degree temperatures the next, and you need to be prepared for all of it.

I dress in layers each day because it is easy to shed layers as needed, and I carry extra outer layers to put on as the weather dictates.

Dry socks are going to feel good after this field dressing job! This bull died in the water—just to make things interesting. Knee-high rubber boots are ideal in this situation.

Starting with the outerwear, I want it to be in camouflage colors. I also want it to be soft and quiet, as well as waterproof. Therefore, all of my outerwear is actually lightweight GORE-TEX rain gear with a soft-nap outer shell.

Since I am usually the one who handles a decoy, I like a dark-brown camouflage pattern. I generally choose Mossy Oak brand clothing because the shades that particular company uses lean toward the darker woodland colors.

For outerwear pants, I prefer bib-type overalls, so if the weather is cold or rainy, that much more of my skin is constantly protected. With bib pants, I can wear a waist-length jacket with a drawstring around the waist, which leaves less material hanging down to snag on underbrush and blow downs. My back is covered no matter what position I am in, sitting or standing.

I also wear Scent-Lok gloves and a facemask. The gloves are not so much for warmth as they are to cover up my white hands, and the mask serves the same purpose.

I carry all of my outerwear in a scent-proof bag in the back of my truck. I put it on each time we get out to start a hunt, and shed it when we get back to the vehicle. This keeps the day-to-day smells that I may pick up to a minimum.

What I wear under my outerwear depends on the weather forecast each day. On a typical day, with frost in the morning and temperatures reaching sixty to seventy degrees by mid-day, I find that I can get away with wearing only a Scent-Lok suit underneath. These suits are warm, but they breathe, and I have yet to be uncomfortable with this setup.

If it is going to rain, or low temperatures are in the forecast, I will put on long johns underneath the Scent-Lok suit. This still allows me to shed a layer should the forecast be wrong.

On those days when the temperatures are going to be unseasonably cold, I not only put on long underwear and the Scent-Lok suit, but also add a pair of camouflage pants over that. The camo pants are kept in another scent-proof bag in the lodge or tent where I am staying. I am a firm believer in the ability of the Scent-Lok style clothing to keep human scent down to a minimum, and I know it is an innovation that has helped me to get inside of what I consider "extremely close range" of over a dozen or so bull moose.

Here in Maine we do not have to wear hunter orange during our moose hunt unless we are carrying firearms. Since I am guiding, I do not fall under that category. In New Brunswick, Canada, however, all members of the party are required to wear hunter orange, so when I am there, I wear an orange vest and hat in compliance with the law and treat them as I do my other outerwear: I store them in a scent-proof bag between hunts.

The kind of footwear I put on each morning depends on the type of terrain I will be hunting, but I am a big fan of GORE-TEX lined hunting boots and I have several pair for different conditions. The use of nylon and GORE-TEX makes these hiking-style boots very friendly on the feet—almost as comfortable as sneakers—yet they will take you from warm weather to cold, and they are extremely water repellent.

Guide Tim Buskirk and his successful hunting party waded into the Allagash Waterway to retrieve this nice bull.

For those areas I hunt that are wet, I like a knee-high rubber boot. There are many brands out on the market, and they come both insulated and non-insulated. I wear the insulated type, as my feet tend to get cold, but if you have no problem with cold feet, go for the non-insulated. They are usually lighter in weight, thus easier to walk in.

Whether you are going to spend your entire day walking or be in and out of a vehicle on short hunts, carry extra socks with you. Changing socks in the middle of the day can be a comfort to your feet, and it will make you feel like you can go on forever. If your feet do get wet because you chose to wear the wrong boots, the dry socks will give you a whole new perspective and feeling of comfort.

I would also recommend that if you are going to be in a boat, truck, or what have you, throw in an extra pair of boots. Wet boots do not do much to keep your spirits up all day, and excessive walking in wet boots may cause blisters.

Hunting from a canoe or watercraft is a little different. Often, hunting by canoe means sitting still with no physical exertion except when paddling. Depending on the weather, this can get mighty cold. I recommend an oversize jacket that can be slipped on and off quickly or just draped over the shoulders for added warmth. If you have to get out of the canoe for short walks, you'll want to shed this heavy layer to keep from sweating.

Getting in and out of a canoe all day can make for wet feet, which is why, if I know that my walks are going to be short in distance, I like to wear a pair of hip boots. They are tough to move in, but they keep feet dry.

And occasionally, if I know my excursions from the watercraft are going to be a distance, I will wear those knee-high rubber boots—and make sure that I carry at least two pairs of spare socks with me.

I want to stress the importance of wearing a life jacket when being on the water, especially when you are wearing heavy boots and multiple layers of clothing. Boots filled with water and soaked clothing are the equivalent of wearing an anchor! ■

14
EQUIPMENT

The equipment a hunting party carries is going to vary greatly, depending on the hunting method. For example, there are items you need while hunting from a truck that would be of no use to you while hunting from a canoe.

Over the years and through personal experience, one thought remains: You can never have too much equipment. No matter what happens or what you have, you will need whatever you left back at home three hundred miles away. Go prepared!

WHAT YOU NEED TO CARRY AT ALL TIMES

I have a medium size fanny pack that goes with me on all hunts. In this pack, aside from the various urines and scents I mentioned before, I carry a number of useful and, what I consider, required items for any moose hunt:

- A spare compass (you never know when you will lose one)
- Two folding hunting knives (nothing dulls a knife quicker than moose hide)
- A folding saw with a blade capable of cutting both wood and bone
- At least one roll of fluorescent surveyor tape
- A one hundred-foot coil of clothesline rope (which I use to hold a moose's legs up while field dressing)
- A bottle of water with a squirt top (I have something to drink and can use it to imitate a cow urinating)
- A flashlight (many times I don't come out of the woods until after dark)
- One spare pair of socks
- A pair of small two-way radios (very handy for keeping in communication with a hunter should I have to leave him during a calling sequence; they eliminate the guesswork when you are separated and not sure what is happening)
- A camouflage face paint compact (in case someone forgets a facemask or gloves back in the vehicle)
- A fluorescent-orange hat and bandanna
- An extra moose call

Even with the urines and scents in it, this pack weighs less than five pounds, and every item is where I can find it when I need it. Additionally, the pack can be put on and taken off quickly, and I do not have to worry about getting stuff out of jacket pockets if I decide to go without my jacket.

This is usually the gear I carry in a daypack on every hunt.

There is one more piece of equipment that Corey and I have found to be indispensable: a hearing enhancement aid. We use the Walker's line of Game Ear products and we are extremely happy with their performance. Corey likes the Game Ear that fits inside of and behind the ear like a hearing aid. I use Walker's Quad Power Muffs. They are a little bulkier, but I can quickly hand them off to a hunter so that he can hear what I am hearing.

My first experience with the hearing enhancement aids was prior to the hunting season, when I was trying to get some film of moose while using a decoy. My cameraman and I parked the truck, walked a short distance and began calling. The cameraman was wearing a pair of the Walker's Power Muffs. I had never tried them, figuring my hearing was just fine.

I had called for about twenty minutes or so and decided it was time to move to a new spot. I turned to leave and noticed my cameraman had the camera set up. Puzzled, I waved my hand in a "Come on, let's get out of here" gesture.

He pointed to his Walker's Muffs and then pointed into the woods to tell me he heard something. I kind of scowled at him but stood there listening. Still hearing nothing, I turned to him and again signaled it was time to leave. He took his muffs off and handed them to me.

Putting them on, I did not have to listen very hard to hear a bull grunting. I could even hear that he was coming at a fast clip and grunting with each step. I took the muffs off, handed them back to the cameraman and listened, but still could not hear him. It was a good twenty minutes before I could hear the bull even faintly coming toward me.

We finally got some film of the bull, and as we headed back to the truck, the cameraman told me he had heard the bull respond to my first call. The total time it took for me to hear the bull without the hearing enhancement device was more than forty minutes. That one episode made a believer out of me. Since then I never venture out moose hunting without my Quad Power Muffs. I know that they have helped me get several moose that I would not have heard without them.

EQUIPMENT FOR EXTENDED HUNTS

On hunts that take me away from my vehicle for an extended period of time such as a full morning hunt. I carry my fanny pack plus a small backpack with some additional gear. In this backpack I carry the following items:

- An additional pair of extra socks
- A sharpening stone
- Four cheesecloth bags that will hold quarters of moose, plus two additional bags for meat cut from the rib cage and neck
- A ten-foot by ten-foot tarp for keeping meat clean
- Heavy card stock tags to use to tag each piece of the moose (if required by law)
- Extra bottles of water
- A fifty-foot coil of 3/8-inch rope to hang quarters of moose if needed
- An inexpensive pair of rain pants (which I'll wear if I have to cut a moose up in the woods; they keep blood from getting on my hunting clothes)
- A roll of paper towels
- A couple of garbage bags for cleaning up

All of these items fit nicely into a medium-size backpack and still leave room to carry lunch and other items, like a camera and film. The pack I favor has outside

This is my backpack gear or—as I like to call it—my cut-up kit. Everything I need to quarter a moose and take care of the meat is here.

This moose was dragged for a bit and then loaded into a truck. A come-a-long hauled the moose into the truck's bed while others lifted its head up. Having the right equipment makes the job easier.

carry straps that I use to store rolled-up hunting clothes, whether items I take off during the hunt or a change I decide to bring along for later use. My pack also has quick-release buckles so I can shed it quickly and put it back on with ease.

IN-THE-TRUCK EQUIPMENT

Hunting from a truck or other 4x4 vehicle usually means you will be able to transport a moose in one piece. If you happen to get your moose someplace where you can reach him with a vehicle, the proper equipment will make this go a lot smoother.

Rope is cheap if you buy it from distributors or other vendors that deal in volume. I carry a two hundred-yard spool of 5/8-inch rope—the kind that is made for the commercial fishing industry. It has a very high tensile strength and a very low stretch factor. I store it in a plastic garbage can and keep the tag ends tied to outside handles. It feeds out of the can with no snarls.

I also carry several pieces of the same rope in various lengths I have picked up over the years, from fifty to one hundred fifty feet long. The extra rope saves me from having to cut my two hundred-yard piece should I need something shorter.

A two-ton come-a-long cable winch is indispensable when trying to load a moose into a truck bed or onto a trailer. I carry two large blocks or pulleys—when you have a couple of hundred yards of rope strung out, it helps to get it up high—to keep the moose from digging into the ground as you are trying to tow it with your vehicle. As the moose gets close to the block, you simply reposition the block closer to the truck. These blocks come in handy if you have to route the rope; they allow you to pull a longer distance with your truck instead of short hitches.

Make sure when you acquire your blocks that they are of sufficient size and strength for what you plan on doing with them. The ones I use will handle one-inch diameter rope, and the sheaves are eight inches in diameter. I have never even heard these pulleys creak when in use.

I also carry a chain saw for moving downed trees that might be in the way when I'm getting a moose out. (Never cut down live trees unless you have the landowner's permission.)

Loading a moose into the bed of a pickup truck can be a chore, even with the help of a cable winch and a couple of big burly guys. A friend of mine showed me a way to make it go easier: He cuts a piece of 3/4-inch plywood to fit between the wheel wells of the truck and in the bed with the tailgate closed. He has a beefed-up connection point at the head of the bed where the hoist is attached. He sets the plywood on the tailgate so that it extends up above the lowered tailgate by about one-third of the overall length of the plywood.

As he winches the moose up the plywood, the plywood levers down once more than half the animal's weight is on the extended part, lifting the moose level with the bed. It is a relatively simple task at this point for three men to slide the plywood with the moose on it into the truck the rest of the way.

Laying the plywood in the back of the truck and placing all your gear on it takes up no room, and this little trick has saved me a lot of aggravation over the years.

Since I do not wear my outerwear in the truck when traveling between hunting locations, I have a plastic storage box that is water tight and large enough to hold my scent-proof bag of clothing. This helps keep things dry. If you get a box that's large enough, you can also store spare boots and other gear in it.

I know other guides and hunters who carry additional gear with them in the truck. One hunter I know carries a battery-operated reciprocal saw for splitting a moose down the backbone like a butcher would. If you feel you might need it, find a place for it. You will not regret it.

EQUIPMENT FOR HUNTING FROM A CANOE

When hunting from a canoe, you are going to be limited in what you can take along. You can carry the items I listed for the fanny pack and the extended hunts and be all set for getting your trophy out of the woods in pieces. To make your canoe- hunting experience more comfortable and ease the chore of getting a moose out, I would make sure to carry a few additional items:

Canoe seats can be very uncomfortable for a full day's hunt. Make sure you bring either floatation cushions or some other type of cushion to sit on. It will keep you from constantly fidgeting. A seat that attaches to the canoe seat and has a back on is going to be even more comfortable; being able to lean back and relax will make for a much more enjoyable day.

Even though you may be wearing or carrying hip boots with you, I would throw in a pair of chest waders. One season, Corey had a hunter shoot a moose that died in water deeper than the hip boots the hunter had brought with him. He had to wade out and spend the next hour caping and quartering the moose while waist deep in cold October water.

I would carry a come-along and a length of rope fifty- to one hundred-feet long as well. If you do get a moose that dies in the water, you may be able to winch him to drier ground, which will make field dressing and caping that much easier. ■

15
TAKING CARE
OF YOUR MOOSE

O nce you have your moose down on the ground, the work really begins. How you decide to remove him from the woods will depend on many factors. The type of vehicle you have, the moose's distance from it, the equipment you have at your disposal, and even weather conditions are all going to influence your decision.

Hunting moose in many locations across North America means hunting near or on logging roads and trails. Often a hunting party will be able to get a vehicle to well within a few hundred yards of a downed moose, and can usually get the animal out in one piece by simply having enough ropes and pulleys.

Then there are those moose that just do not want to die anywhere near a road, and they will run in the opposite direction from a road to die. Such moose are going to require that you cut them into pieces to get them out of the woods—and keep in mind that a moose hunt during the rut usually means warm weather. That, too, may be a factor in deciding whether or not to cut your moose into pieces.

FIELD DRESSING

Moose hide is very thick and will retain the animal's body heat. The quicker you can cool the meat, the better its quality for your table, and the less chance you will have of spoilage.

Be very careful when field dressing if you are going to have a head mount made of a moose. Never slit the throat, as many old timers will tell you. Without the heart pumping, you will not drain any additional blood from the animal by slitting the throat. All you do is bleed out the immediate area of the cut.

Drain the blood from the animal as you remove the entrails; blood left in the carcass at this point will be drained when it is hung up. In the case of having to quarter the animal, which is good to do in extremely warm weather, blood will drain from the meat as you quarter the moose and hang the quarters.

When I field dress a moose for a client who tells me he plans to do a head mount of the animal, I stop my cut at the bottom of the sternum. This means I have to literally get into the animal and reach up into the chest cavity to remove the heart and lungs. A long-blade knife, and having no qualms about getting blood on yourself, from your wrists to your shoulders, makes this go much easier.

If a client tells me he is going to have an antler mount or a European mount made, then I have no problem taking my bone saw and splitting the chest all the

Bernard and I prepare a moose for field dressing. Note how one side of the moose is propped up with rope secured around a tree.

way to the neck. This makes removing the heart and lungs a much simpler task, and keeps the gutter a lot cleaner. But if you do this on a moose destined to be a head and shoulder mount, you may very well have a taxidermist calling you every name in the book as he sews up three additional feet of hide. Do not expect him to do you any favors in the very near future!

If you are in a situation where you may not be able to reach a meat cooler or butcher for twelve or more hours, it may be advisable to remove the hide and quarter the moose. To someone who has never had the experience of cutting a moose in quarters, it can be an intimidating task, but it is not really that difficult. I can cape and quarter a moose by myself in about three hours; Corey and I working together have been known to take care of a moose in slightly over an hour. The most critical factor in caping and quartering a moose is making sure you have enough knives handy for the chore, or a good set of sharpening stones. Nothing dulls a knife quicker than moose hair.

With the moose lying on its side, start by making cuts up the back of the front legs, from behind the knee to the brisket. On the side that is up, continue the cut from the brisket up over the shoulder, and end your cut at the backbone. Make another cut following the backbone toward the skull, stopping at the base of the skull. Make one more cut at the intersection or your two cuts down the backbone toward the tail. You can now skin the leg and shoulder for your cape. Work the hide off the leg, over the shoulder, and up the neck to the base of the skull. Continue skinning and rolling the hide away toward the backbone.

The front shoulder will now be bare of hide and can be separated from the body with just a knife. Pushing the leg up as high as you can, cut the meat and tendons, following the rib cage until you come to the shoulder blade. Slip your knife between the shoulder blade and the ribs and it will pop right away. Now hang the quarter, or lay it out on the tarp. If flies are a problem, now is a good time to put it into the cheesecloth bag.

You can now work the second piece of hide from the back of the ribs to the hind end of the moose. You should have already made a cut in the rear leg, as you did on the front leg, from the back of the knee area to the rectum of the moose.

Again, you will expose the rear leg of hide. Removing the rear leg is similar to removing the front leg, except that as you work your knife through the meat, be feeling for a ball-and-socket joint. Slip the blade of your knife between the ball and socket and the rear leg will pop right off. Take care of this as you did the front quarter.

With the upside of the rib cage exposed, you can now trim all the meat from the ribs. Remove the loin or back strap from the back as well, so you can keep it clean.

To remove the loin, work your knife along the backbone from the front shoulder to the hind end. Follow the backbone closely so as not to lose any meat. Move back to the front end and insert your knife from the base of the neck, following the

The knife points to the rear leg ball joint. Once this is found and cut away from surrounding tissue, the hindquarter will fall right off with nothing more than some trimming with a knife.

ribs, into the backbone. Once the two cuts come together, you will have a slab of loose meat that you can lift up and roll back. Continue to work your knife along the ribs and the backbone, rolling the slab of meat away as you work. If you have help, let another person pull the meat up as you cut. It is the easiest way to do it.

I usually take all the meat cut from the ribs and place it in one cheesecloth bag for burger or stew meat, and place the loins into a separate bag so it doesn't end up as burger by mistake.

At this point, you have cleaned one side of the moose and are now ready to do the other side. With a little effort, you can roll the moose over and repeat the

Darrell Richards reaches into the chest cavity of a moose to remove the heart and lungs. Note how the legs are tied back. The chest/ribs were not split on this moose as the hunter wanted to preserve the hide for a head mount.

process. When you are done, you will have the four quarters, a bag of rib meat, and another bag of meat from the loins. The neck has a substantial amount of meat, so take the time to bone it out. You can either put it into the burger-meat bag or in the bag with the loins, as I do (since I prefer to make roasts from it).

You can successfully cape and quarter a moose without having to remove the guts from the animal. However, you lose the best piece of meat, the inside loins or tenderloins, as they are called. To remove these, you must take out the viscera. The tenderloins are located at the lower end of the rib cage along the inner backbone; there is one on either side, and you remove them as you did the outer loins, only these are smaller.

If you have taken your time and removed all of the rib meat and neck meat from the carcass, a raven will have a hard time making a meal out of what you leave behind.

Once you have the cape portion of the hide skinned away from the body, you can cut through the neck of the moose at the base of the skull. To accomplish this, work your knife between the skull and the first vertebra or use a bone saw and simply cut through the neck bone—what I refer to as woods caping; the hide is still attached to the skull and antlers. This can now be rolled up and made ready for transportation out of the woods. If flies are a problem, place the cape and skull into a cheesecloth bag and tie it tight around the antlers.

If you don't have a bag of sufficient size, you may opt for the pepper method of keeping the flies at bay: I purchase an institutional size can of black pepper—the kind that weighs a pound or more and is available at all of the discount-club outlets.

I first dust the eyes and ears liberally with black pepper, and then I pack pepper into the nostrils. Laying the hide out flesh side up, I dust it with pepper as well, paying close attention to the meat that may be still attached to the hide. It will keep the flies off until you get it to a cold storage locker or your local taxidermist.

If I am removing a moose from the woods in one piece, I also dust the head orifices with pepper, and pack any bullet holes with pepper as well, to keep some of the flies away.

If I do decide to bring a moose out of the woods in one piece, I still want to make sure to cool the meat—especially if the weather is warm. Do not be afraid to

Rick Dodge (left) and a very happy hunter. This bull was killed several miles back in the woods and had to be quartered to get it out. With such a large rack and the great distance in getting it out, Rick decided to complete cape out the head to lighten the load.

put some bags of ice inside the body cavity, although I have found the best method of cooling a moose carcass down is to use frozen jugs of water.

Before going on your moose hunt, freeze twenty or more two-liter bottles of water. If you are going off on a hunt where no electricity is available, pack as many frozen jugs as you can in spare coolers. When you have the moose loaded on your truck, pack as many of the bottles as you can inside the body cavity. It will cool the meat and keep some flies away.

If electricity is available at your camp, I have found that carrying a small freezer in my truck bed, filled with the frozen water jugs, makes sense. You can plug the freezer in once or twice a day to keep the jugs frozen solid, and once you have your moose butchered, it gives you a place to store some of the meat for your ride home.

I want to pass along some of the problems I have seen in bringing a moose out whole from the woods, and ways to resolve them.

If you have to drag a moose more than three hundred yards, you are probably going to lose a considerable amount of hair from the hide just from rubbing, so avoid this at all costs if you plan to have a head mount done.

To avoid scraping off hair when dragging the carcass, raise the head and chest up off the ground. The best way to do this is to use an ATV and tie the head to the top of the rear luggage rack. That will lift enough of the cape area off the ground so you have minimal hair rub.

If you cannot use an ATV, you may want to consider sliding something under the neck and chest portion of the moose to protect the hide. The best object I have found for this is the hood of an old Volkswagen Beetle. Laying the forward body section of a moose in the VW hood and securely lashing it in will protect the hide and make sliding the moose out of the woods that much easier.

Taxidermists like to do as little sewing as possible when making a mount. The more sewing involved the more time it takes. Also, there is the chance of not getting the hide to match up perfectly. I have heard this is especially true when hunters use a chainsaw to cut moose into quarters. I even saw a video that showed a chainsaw being used to aid in field dressing a moose. Please do not do this! You will lose a lot of meat to waste as bone chips produced by the saw end up all through the exposed meat. A saw also produces a huge pile of meat scraps, and unless it is perfectly clean, all that meat will be spread around the exposed meat as well and this will be the first meat to go bad and start the process for other meat it lands on to go bad.

There is nothing wrong with using a bone saw or a reciprocating saw that has a bone blade in it. Butchers use this when slicing a moose down the backbone. It leaves very few chips and the teeth are fine enough to cut meat without a lot of waste.

Tanya Albert puts on the final touches to a moose mount in her studio in Millinocket, Maine.

TROPHY CARE

Every year I hear of horror stories from hunters or taxidermists of moose capes that cannot be made into mounts due to spoilage of the hide. As a hide starts to go bad and rot, the hair begins to slip off, and nothing can be done to reverse this once it occurs. The hunter is now relegated to having an antler mount or using a cape from another moose other than the one he killed.

If you take care of your cape, you will not have a problem. Get it to a taxidermist within twelve to sixteen hours of the kill if you have no refrigeration available. If you plan on transporting your cape a distance to your own local taxidermist, get it into a freezer so that you can transport it frozen.

Tanya Albert of Albert's Taxidermy in Millinocket, Maine, offers this advice to moose hunters:

1. Get the hide off the moose as soon as possible.

2. Get the cape and skull to the taxidermist you are going to use as soon as possible, if not sooner.

3. If you cannot get the cape to your taxidermist, get it into a cold-storage facility as soon as you can.

4. If you are planning on taking the cape to your taxidermist, and it is going to be a six- to ten-hour ride or more, have the cape and skull frozen. Carry it inside a vehicle and do not lay it on a trailer uncovered, exposed to the sun.

5. If you have to travel any distance with your cape, build a plywood box with a lid that will hold the cape and skull, with the antlers attached. Put some drain holes in the bottom of the box and then build a framework to keep the cape off the bottom. Cover the cape with a tarp or plastic wrap and pack it on ice. Packing a cape and skull this way will allow you to travel a considerable distance without it going bad. A box that measures five-feet wide by four-feet long by three-and-a-half-feet tall will suffice in most cases. ■

16
WEAPONS FOR MOOSE HUNTING

By now it has been established in this book that moose are very large game animals. To take a mature bull moose down, particularly with one shot, demands a key element by the hunter—quality shot placement on an animal that is preferably standing broadside. The next crucial factor is to be sure that the firearm used is one that a hunter has plenty of experience shooting and is totally comfortable and confident using.

On any big-game hunt, including a moose hunt, it is wise to practice with the firearm or bow-hunting equipment that will be used. When you book a moose hunt, ask the outfitter what he expects the average shot distance to be; they are more than willing to share this information. Practice at that distance as often as is practical before leaving for your hunt. It is also wise to practice shooting at further distances as well. For instance, if the outfitter tells you the average shot will be 100 yards, make sure you are also capable of shooting accurately at double that distance. Remember this: consistently successful big-game hunters are extremely aware of their shooting capabilities. All good shooters know their maximum effective range. It is much better to let a bull moose walk off than to shoot at him at a distance you're not comfortable with or haven't practiced at. Although it can get costly, always practice with the exact ammunition you plan to use on the hunt. In the end, doing this will pay off in big dividends.

It can't be over emphasized how important shooting sticks are on a big-game hunt. They will increase accuracy ten-fold. However, a hunter must practice with shooting sticks long before the hunt. The practice will provide familiarity, which in turn will deliver confidence when shooting from sticks. While it is not recommended to shoot without a good rest, shooting off-hand may indeed come into play. If it does, it is best to be prepared to do so confidently. Practicing shooting off-hand is a good idea but should only be used if there is absolutely nothing to rest your firearm on and an off-hand shot is the last resort.

Once all the above elements are met, only then does bullet choice and caliber come into play. For the sole sake of demonstrating our experience I mention the following: I have hunted all types of big game for over fifty years across North America and Africa. For the last thirty-two years, my wife Kate and I have hosted our television show and have used every imaginable caliber and ammunition type in taking big game over that period of time. Our son, Peter (aka Cody) began his big-game hunting at ten years old (in places where it was legal). Cody is well versed in all aspects of firearms and ammunition and co-hosts a firearm and ammo segment on *Woods N' Water Big Game Adventures*. Between us we have amassed more than 100 years of experience shooting big game. Again, I mention this only to demonstrate our years of familiarity regarding what calibers and ammunition have proven to be successful year after year for the three of us.

We feel, as many experienced big-game hunters, guides, and outfitters do, that any of today's firearms starting at a .270 WSM and going larger, matched with a bullet weighing 150 grains or more, are definitely capable of taking down moose. The flatter a rifle shoots the better for a moose hunt.

Over the years we have used all types of bullets and loads. One of our favorite bullets is the Winchester XP3. During several moose hunts in Newfoundland, I have taken several mature bulls using a .270 WSM with 150 grain Winchester XP3s. My wife Kate has also taken several bulls using a .308 with 150 grain XP3s. Cody has took his big bull using a .300 WSM using 180 grain XP3s. The performance of the XP3 bullet has been extraordinary. All the bulls we have taken were killed with one well-placed shot (you can see these hunts on YouTube under "Peter Fiduccia Woods N' Water"). Other premium bullets include Winchester Ballistic Silvertips, E-tips. Shoot the ammo you are most comfortable with or, better stated, the ammunition your rifle shoots best—just make sure they are the premium bullets a particular manufacturer offers.

I want to be clear that any quality ammunition will perform equally well. The point being made here is that bullet and load choices are crucial when considering a moose hunt. The savvy hunter spends a little more money to use premium ammunition to practice and hunt with in order to assure success. Realistically, most ammunition will work equally well as long as it delivers the required amount of down-range energy. The fact is, no matter what caliber is used—from a .270 WSM and up—as long as the hunter has properly sighted it in, practiced with it, and can shoot with a maximum amount of confidence, the combined elements will do the job of taking a moose to the ground.

While some hunters choose to shoot some of the "heavy" calibers including the .300 .338, .45-70 Government, or .444 Marlin, most seasoned ballistic gurus, guides, and skilled hunters know these super large and magnum calibers are basically "over kill" when it comes to taking moose. Yes, they can definitely get the job done, but at the risk of being too much gun for most hunters to shoot without flinching, and therefore, most are not able to shoot them consistently and accurately. Most guides recommend heavier calibers (or the "magnums") only if the hunter is experienced with them and able to "handle the recoil."

It is common knowledge that some guides like their hunters to shoot large calibers with heavy loads, and they go as far as to recommend they use magnum calibers. However, their main reason for this is that they don't want a client to wound a moose and chance losing the animal. Not a wise concept, as the shooter is much more likely to wound and lose a bull, or even miss it entirely, when using a heavy caliber than he or she would if shooting a smaller caliber that can be handled without flinching, such as the highly underrated .308 cartridge. To see over a dozen one-shot kills of animals including moose, caribou, bear, deer, and antelope taken with .270 WSM, .308, and a .30-06, visit YouTube and click on "Peter Fiduccia's Woods N' Water" and then search "one-shot kills."

The heaviest caliber most seasoned moose guides recommend is the .300 WSM. It is formidable, performs accurately, and delivers less recoil than its brawnier cousins do. The reduced recoil makes any firearm enormously more efficient than it would be with the really large calibers. This is particularly true for youngsters, some small-framed women and men, and for inexperienced moose hunters.

Here are the key elements to accurate shooting and putting a moose down in his tracks:

- The old adage "practice makes perfect" should always be applied to any big-game hunt, particularly an expensive guided hunt. Practice enough with your firearm *before* leaving to ensure confidence when you place the crosshairs on your bull moose. One well-placed shot will drop the largest of bulls in his tracks.
- Never skimp on buying your ammunition. When the cost of a few boxes of high performing ammo is matched up to the cost of a guided hunt, perhaps of a once-in-a-lifetime moose hunt, buying cheap ammunition doesn't make any sense at all.
- Always shoot the *exact* same type of ammunition on the hunt that you practiced with before leaving.
- Using less than quality optics (scopes and binoculars) is often the cause of a hunt ending badly. It is better to save for an extra year in order to buy quality optics like Swarovski than to risk using cheaply made optics for a high-cost big-game hunt.
- As soon as possible after arriving at camp always sight-in your firearm. You'll hate yourself if you don't. The odds are the gun will be "on." However, if it is not, it is better to find out before you go hunting rather than discovering it after you shoot at a big bull and either miss or wound it. Not sighting-in at camp has been a major cause of hunts going badly.
- Remember that a poor shooting ability or worse yet, a badly placed shot can't be rectified by using larger calibers.
- Know your range shooting limitations and stay within them without diversion.
- Never shoot a moose in its "hump." The hump is nothing more than gristle and meat. Hit high in the hump a moose will either stumble or drop, but more times than not he will recover quickly and run off.
- Try to avoid shooting a moose facing directly at you. If you are even slightly off the center of the chest he will run for a long distance before dying. If hit perfectly square in the chest he will drop in his tracks.
- Most experienced guides and experienced hunters will confirm the best shot to bring a moose down instantly is in the neck, a sizeable target on a bull-

moose. If you hit the spine, death is instantaneous. If you miss the spine and hit the major arteries, it will cause severe arterial damage and the bull will quickly die.

- If a moose drops on bullet impact, don't take your sights off him. You want to prevent him from getting back to his feet. Although unfortunately, the general consensus of professional guides is to "put as many bullets into him as you have to keep him down." I totally disagree with this advice. Keep your gun pointed at the moose and be totally prepared to take a quick follow-up shot if necessary. That requires never taking your sights off the moose until it is absolutely confirmed that he is dead. Filling a moose with holes unnecessarily ends up ruining a lot of prime-tasting meat. Moose meat is the best tasting venison by far. If he makes the slightest effort to get up, then shoot him again.

- As with any big-game animal the hunter should always try to determine the animal's reaction when shot; it will provide priceless clues if a blood trail has to be followed.

By following these guidelines and suggestions you will insure yourself a safe, enjoyable, and successful hunt.

TROPHY MOOSE AND
WHAT MAKES A TROPHY

What makes a moose a trophy? This is one of the most common questions when it comes to moose hunting. It came up during my interview with Karen Morris, the State of Maine Moose Research leader, and it always comes as the moose hunters arrive in camp the night before the season opens. Everyone wants to know what would be a trophy.

In my interview with Karen, I asked her what Maine officials considered a trophy moose as portrayed in the literature put out for the benefit of moose hunters in the state. She laughed and gave me two answers that make total sense.

"A trophy is what the hunter considers a trophy, not some numbers in a book," she said. When I pressed her about the language in the Maine Moose Hunter's Information Guide, she told me that I would have to talk to the Information and Education Director about what was written in the guide, but she did allude to the fact that the information contained in that state-distributed booklet was based on moose with palmed antlers. It was a theory I had for years, but I was never able to get a straight answer from officials. To me, Karen's first definition is the most accurate one. A trophy is what the hunter makes of it.

A trophy or not? Judging by the smiles on the party's faces, I would say yes—and end to a successful New Brunswick moose hunt.

MOOSE HUNTING

My first Maine moose is still, in my mind, a trophy. It was forty-nine inches wide and had double paddles, or shovels—one brow paddle with four points and the other with five points. The bull had nineteen points total and weighed 1,004 pounds—all of which, for me, add up to it being a true trophy.

We had a muzzleloader hunter one year who was with one of my best guides. On opening morning, the hunter chose to pass on a moose that would have made the Maine Skull and Antler Club in the muzzleloading class. The hunter and guide hunted hard the rest of the week in a zone that was considered to be not that productive. On Friday, the hunter killed a small bull that was measured in points and not width, and he could not have been more pleased when he talked to me at season's end.

Explaining why he chose to pass on the first moose, he said that it would have been too easy to kill on opening morning. Even though the guide did his job as expected and called the bull in within easy range, the hunter wanted to wait. He was almost apologetic about choosing the smaller bull, but he said that to him, it was more of a trophy, because he had hunted all week for it.

George Perry once guided a hunter who videotaped twenty-seven moose from Monday through Friday. I hunted with George and the hunter the second half of the week, and on Thursday afternoon I called in the largest bull that I had ever called in; there was no doubt in my mind or George's that the moose would have been a new state record. He was well over sixty inches, and the points outlining his paddles were in excess of ten inches on average. At one point during the hunt, I was less than thirty feet from the bull and had a completely unobstructed view of him. The hunter, who had an easy quartering-away shot at less than one hundred feet, was using a .338 Winchester Magnum.

After the whole fiasco went down without a shot being fired, I was dumbfounded and George was shaking his head in disbelief. But the hunter had a huge smile on his face, and he said that he had never seen anything so impressive as the size of that moose and the way I talked him right in. He told George and me that he did not want to shoot the animal back-to, while it was trotting away.

On the last day of the moose hunt, at 10 o'clock in the morning, that hunter took a well-palmed bull that only measured thirty-five inches. He harvested the bull with three shots from his .338 Winchester Magnum at over two hundred yards. Normally, I would not let the average hunter take such a shot, but this being the last day of the season, I felt it was time for a Hail Mary play.

The hunter hit that moose three times in an area you could cover with a baseball. He was all smiles, as were George and I. Our hunter had his moose, and we had our one hundred percent success rate for the year.

After the obligatory handshakes and back slaps at the kill site, I complimented the hunter on his shooting. He smiled again and asked me if I knew what he had done for a living before he retired. I told him no; all I knew was that he had been a government employee. He then informed George and me that he had worked as a shooting instructor with the United States Army. He had not lied to us; he just failed to give a total job description.

These successful hunters flew into a remote area for their hunt. The moose was quartered and flown out along with the hunters (which took two trips!). The fly-in part of the trip made this animal a trophy for them.

We found out later through other hunters and outfitters that he frequently takes hunting trips around the world, and spends the entire trip videotaping animals, not shooting. He has even done this in Africa. Then, on the last day of his hunt, he takes whatever animals present themselves to him. He gauges his trophies not on what he has taken, but rather on his tapes and memories of the hunts. The thing that amazed me is that the man was set to go home at noontime with no moose, and completely happy with his experience.

On the other end of the spectrum, there was a hunter I had a few years back. Early in the hunt, he missed a truly remarkable bull with a rifle. It was not because the moose was long way off; the shot he had was thirty yards. At that distance, he not only missed the bull once, but twice, as it was standing broadside.

I somehow managed to call the bull back after the second miss so that he could shoot at it again, only this time at a closer range that I measured in feet, not yards. Two more standing shots at less than thirty feet and one more at about forty feet, and that bull was now filed away under the highly educated category. Five shots on one moose, and somehow the hunter managed to miss each time. I am sure "Moose Fever" played a major role in the display of marksmanship we all witnessed that morning.

The next day, his partner on the same license killed a bull with a bow. It was a very nice bull and would have made the Maine record books, if not Pope and Young as well.

The hunter from the day before walked up to the dead arrow-shot moose, kicked it and muttered obscenities the entire time that we guides and the killer of the moose were all high-fiving each other. He totally took away from the experience for all of us present.

While it was the largest bull I ever have called in for a bow hunter to harvest to date, I still think back on that experience with disgust. The man who missed with a rifle judged a trophy, and a hunt, on what he had failed to do, and not his partner's accomplishment.

One other type of client I have had is what I call a "horn hunter." Horn hunters gauge their success not only on the hunters and their kills in camp, but also on record-

This small bull moose is considered a trophy by the Maine Department of Inland Fisheries and Wildlife because of the palmed antlers. A trophy is what you make of it.

book numbers. I can understand the mentality to want to take a record-book animal; I have taken a B&C-class whitetail, and it is a thrill (do not look for it in the record book; I did not register it). But I have other trophies that are much more memorable due to the facts surrounding the hunts.

I have found over the years that horn hunters or record-book seekers have lost what the hunt is all about: the pitting of wits, skills, and patience against a wild animal in its own natural environment. Couple this with the fact that the hunter usually has a limited amount of time and resources, and you have the makings for a truly memorable hunt—until you throw numbers into it.

In moose camp on orientation night, when I am asked what makes a trophy moose, here is my reply:

"A trophy is what you make of it! If it is a four-point bull that the guide called in to ten feet and you are more than intrigued with the whole process he went through than the fact that this is a trophy. Are you happy with everything that made it a hunt? Did you get out of the vehicle and actually hunt? Did your guide point things out to you? Will you remember how big the animal was, or will you remember your guide's name? Would you want to return to hunt with us again? If you answer yes to these questions, then you decide what a trophy is.

"If you want numbers, here you go. Gun hunters look for a well-palmed set of antlers that is as wide on the inside as the moose is thick through the body across the back. This is going to put you roughly at the forty-five-inch mark. Look for brow palms and not brow points. If he has brow palms with points on them, you are looking at a good moose. More than likely he is over four-and-a-half years of age. If you want a fifty-inch or better bull, check with your guide on each moose. He will be able to guess within a couple of inches.

"Bow hunters look for a well-palmed antler that is not quite as wide on the outside as the moose is thick, body wise, at the shoulder. You will be looking at 38 to forty inches. Look for the height of the antlers to be near the thickness of his body from belly to back. If the rack height is near to two-thirds of his body thickness, with all the other features, you got a moose you can be proud of."

I personally feel that all hunters can stand to take a step back and look at what they consider a trophy. Ask yourself some basic questions, and I certainly hope that numbers and measurements do not come into your answers. If you need to measure your success with numbers, you have totally lost the meaning of hunting. Golf is a game that is measured by numbers. Take it up; you will be a lot happier. ■

18
THE BEST MOOSE-HUNTING DESTINATIONS

Many potential moose hunters want to know the best place to hunt moose. There are many factors that can figure into a decision when you are making preparations.

Almost all of my experience has been in Maine, with a little bit in New Brunswick and New Hampshire. So I put the question to Maryo Pepin, who has hunted moose in his home province of Quebec as well as in New Brunswick, Nova Scotia, Manitoba, Alberta, British Columbia, Newfoundland, the Yukon and the state of Maine.

Maryo told me about places in Quebec that have higher concentrations of moose than are found in Maine, but they have "draw-only" hunts in those locations open just to Quebec residents. For a non-resident to hunt in such a place, he or she must be under a resident who has drawn a tag for the area. The draw-only areas are also very small. To give me a better understanding of their size, Maryo said

Maryo Pepin calls for moose in Newfoundland, Canada.

it would be like taking Zone 1 in Maine, which is about 1,420 square miles, and dividing it into twenty smaller sections—which makes the size of the draw zones around seventy square miles. If you get a draw area in Quebec where no moose are present during your hunt, you are out of luck.

Newfoundland has lots of moose, and the price is reasonable for a hunt as well, generally running around $3,000. Hunting techniques there differ from other regions. For example, not every guide is a moose caller, since some Newfoundlanders find it much more effective to push moose for their clients or still-hunt with them. This does not keep a person in one spot very long; everyone is moving, and many moose are sighted.

The key word is sighted, not killed. While most Newfoundland moose hunts run at a one hundred percent success rate, one look at the average size of the ani-mals and you will quickly see that, with a few exceptions, a Newfoundland hunt is a meat hunt rather than a trophy hunt. Many of the moose I have seen taken there were in the forty-inch or under class.

Maryo has hunted in Newfoundland twice, and both times he found that the moose were very susceptible to calling. On one particular trip, he called in twen-ty-three bulls in four days. He made his kill early in the week and spent a couple of days calling for other guests of the lodge where he was staying.

I want to go to Newfoundland for my own experience, just to be able to call

This four bulls were taken by members of the Buck Expert pro staff during an opening morning of the New Brunswick moose hunt.

moose that have not been called to. It will be like hunting back in Maine during the late 1980s and early 1990s.

The Yukon is a moose hunter's Mecca. The largest moose in North America live there, and in Alaska, and a hunter has a chance to take a sixty-five-inch or better moose. But because a moose hunt in such locales often runs $8,000 or more, it is cost prohibitive for most hunters. Maryo said if it were not for the fact that some outfitters want him to come up and train their guides, he would not be able to afford to hunt there.

New Brunswick is a good hunting area, but you need to do your homework before going. Because the hunt is only three days long, the traveling hunter will want to make sure that he has a competent guide with knowledge of the area. Maryo has been fortunate to have hunted New Brunswick with members of his pro-staff who live there. My experiences in New Brunswick have been pleasant and productive as well. I had good guides who knew the area extensively and left the calling to me. We came in contact with moose daily and took some fine animals. A traveling hunter will find that most New Brunswick guides are competent callers.

Maryo feels that Maine is the number-one moose-hunting destination. Large zones, low hunter numbers, the fact that many locals will not get out of their vehicles, and lots of moose make this the place to go. And not only are there lots of moose, but quality moose as well. Having hunted and called in Maine since 1996, a forty-nine- or fifty-inch bull does not get Maryo excited anymore. Moose of this size are a common occurrence.

I have to agree with him. Having hunted moose in Maine since 1980, it takes a bull measuring over fifty-five inches to get me excited these days. I have personally seen a bull measuring sixty-five inches and another measuring sixty-three inches killed in Maine. Forty-five to fifty-inch spreads are great trophy moose by any standards.

As Maryo also said, Maine moose outfitters have no idea of the gold mine they are sitting on. Many guides offer hunts for slightly over $1,000, all inclusive. The same quality of hunt in Newfoundland would be a bargain at $3,000.

Maryo has a wish list of moose hunts he would still like to go on. Russia is at the top, followed by Alaska, and he has also been looking at Sweden as a destination. The sheer number of moose killed in that small country makes it very appealing to him.

Northern New Hampshire, along the borders of Maine, Vermont, and Quebec, offers a high-success rate hunt, and they do take some very large moose there. Darrell Richards has hunted in New Hampshire twice, and both times took a very nice trophy animal in the high forty-inch class.

To the hunter applying for a New Hampshire tag, beware. Moose tags are given throughout the entire state, but there is very little public land in the southern region, and also very little undeveloped land.

I spoke with a moose hunter once who had drawn a tag for an area in southern New Hampshire. He told me that he got a moose, although it was not very large—just four points, he told me. But the real disappointment was where he had to hunt:

MOOSE HUNTING

He and his partner hunted in between a golf course and a housing development. He said that they came in contact with joggers, hikers, and other non-consumptive users who were appalled that they were moose hunting in the area.

Since this hunter was not a resident of New Hampshire and was unfamiliar with the state, he did not know what he was getting into in this southern zone. It pays to do your homework before filling out the draw applications. Find out if you can apply for only certain zones and whether you are going to lose any bonus points, if any are awarded, should you turn down a permit.

Vermont is much the same as New Hampshire. Large trophy-size moose are found in the northern region. In the more built-up areas of the state, a hunter may have a tough time finding an area that lends itself to a quality hunting experience.

Portions of Quebec allow hunters to buy a moose tag over the counter. Be warned, though, that along the Maine-Quebec border, the land that is available for hunting is often under lease agreements with clubs and individuals. Public land in this corridor is at a premium. Also, do not think that just knocking on a few doors will gain you permission to hunt in the area. Moose hunting in Quebec is what whitetail hunting is in the United States Hunting rights to land not leased are often reserved for family members. Again, do your homework before heading across the border to hunt.

Without a doubt, the draw hunts offer your best chances to take a trophy moose in the northeast states and provinces. Lacking success in the draw hunts, the hunter who wishes to go after a moose should think about Newfoundland or, for a once-in-a-lifetime hunt, Alaska. No matter where you choose to go, do the research and make sure that you get the quality of hunt you are looking for. ■

19
MARYO PEPIN

Maryo Pepin has hunted moose in Quebec since the first time he accompanied his father on a moose hunt at the age of fourteen. Killing his first moose at the age of sixteen had him hooked for life.

I met Maryo back in 1999 through Corey Kinney at a sportsman's show, where I saw a video presentation of the effectiveness of the Buck Expert Moose Call. The first time I had a chance to be in a moose camp with Maryo and other members of his pro-staff was, to say the least, an awe-inspiring experience. I thought I knew moose hunting until then. The Buck Expert pro-staff's knowledge, and willingness to share what they knew, all helped make me a better moose hunter.

Over the last few years of having the opportunity to be in the same camps with Maryo, I am still in awe of what he learns each day in the field. After having hunted with him and members of his staff, I felt extremely comfortable in my knowledge

Maryo Pepin with a moose calf. Maryo is one of a few researchers who successfully breed moose in captivity.

Maryo Pepin with a cow at his research center in Quebec.

of moose and moose calling. One night during my third year with these hunters, I realized I had come of age, so to speak, when Maryo asked me what I thought of a particular hunting scenario. He listened intently to my answer and relayed that his observations were the same as mine.

The next year, I told Maryo of an observation I had made during the moose season. He listened, fascinated that I had noticed this phenomenon, and then informed me that he'd heard old-time Quebec moose hunters talk of the same situation. Since that time, he has experimented with my findings and even gone further in-depth. We, as moose guides and hunters, now have another tool in our box of tricks to kill a moose.

Many of the insights you find in this book can be attributed to what Maryo has learned through years of moose hunting and operating the Buck Expert Research Center. During an interview with him for this book, he told me that helping to call moose in Maine with Corey and me and our other guides has made for some very interesting revelations in moose behavior. The fact that he has five to fifteen other moose callers out in the woods during the season, all willing to share information, helps. It means new techniques can be tried not by one man but many, and made those of us associated with Buck Expert able to jump to the forefront of the moose-hunting world.

Maryo founded the Buck Expert Research Center in 1992 with the acquisition of his first moose. The herd grew as a result of his careful breeding program, giving him the wherewithal to collect pure moose urine for the hunting scents and lures market.

In 1995, Maryo came up with the concept of the moose call that he markets today. He tested it in Maine with a friend of his who had drawn a Maine moose tag, and after that first successful hunt, Buck Expert Game Calls was off and running.

If imitation is a form of flattery, then Maryo is flattered. Since the introduction of the Buck Expert moose call, other companies have copied his idea of using an exposed reed. Before he devised his calls, some call-manufacturing companies seemed to have no real idea as to what a moose sounded like, let alone the cow in heat. Now almost every call company has a moose call on the market, and each and every one is built on the exposed-reed concept. Unfortunately for most call companies, they do not have access to a captive moose herd to copy the distinctive sounds made by the male and female moose at different times.

Its moose herd has given Buck Expert a definite advantage over the competition. Maryo attaches microphones to the moose and records their sounds. He then brings the recordings into a sound lab and runs them through a spectrograph on a computer.

He not only has the actual sound, but a printout of it when he sets out to make a call. A Buck Expert call may not be pleasing to human ears, but it will be to the ears of the animals that make such sounds. Animals hear differently from humans!

I have to laugh when I do seminars demonstrating Maryo's calls. I have well-

Maryo Pepin with a bow-killed moose.

known hunters and game-call company representatives come and tell me that the Buck Expert calls do not sound right. When I produce a video and audiotape of sounds made by moose, and then demonstrate the call again, many of those folks either walk off or give a song and dance about how it is captive animal and it will sound different anyway.

I can tell you that I have personally used every moose call made prior to using a Buck Expert call, and I still continue to buy and try out moose calls made by other companies that show up on the market, touting superior qualities. Most do not even make a sound that remotely resembles a moose, let alone a cow in heat.

If the average consumer did some homework before buying a call, he would find out that many call companies do not have access to a captive animal herd, let alone a herd of wild moose, to be able to copy the sounds. Buck Expert's captive herd not only enables the company to make a true-sounding moose call, but also the only true moose urines and musks on the market. Maryo even has broken down the chemical composition of natural urine and copied it into the synthetic urines he now sells.

His success has truly changed the way moose are hunted. In days gone by, many Quebec moose hunters climbed into a tree and started calling. They would sit in the same tree for the entire week and hope that a moose came to them and their calls.

Now, with Maryo's products, which have been tested and proven by guides and hunters like myself, moose hunting has changed, even in Quebec, and hunters report amazing success year after year. Maryo once told me, "In Quebec, moose calling and hunting is not a sport, but a religion." If this is true, then Maryo has to be the head of this church. ■

20
LESTER AND THE GOD RONCHER MOOSE

y great-grandfather, Lester, wrote the following story around 1927. We are not sure if it was ever published in his lifetime or if he wrote it as his own personal memoirs—a way to record what was obviously an unforgettable hunt. We found the story neatly typed in his papers after his death in 1973. At the time, I was twelve years old and had spent a considerable amount of time hunting and trout fishing with my great-grandfather and my Dad at our family camp in T4R3, Maine—Lester's beloved Skiticook Country, where he grew up in the great outdoors.

The story is written as he would have told it. Nothing has been changed from the way he wrote it, and each time I read the story, I can hear his voice. After you read it, maybe you will be able to understand my love of moose hunting.

THE STORY

From the time, very early in my infancy, when I was first bitten in the trigger finger by the hunting bug, it was my deep, definite and continuous ambition to perforate the hide of an

Lester Kelso and his "God Roncher" moose. Even at the time this bull was taken, it was an exceptional trophy. This picture appeared in a few Quebec newspapers and in Maine. The sixty-inch spread and the paddle width are rare. I would like to locate this trophy.

177

old "god-roncher" of a bull moose. About the time I was entering my teens, there was some mighty-fine moose hunting in Aroostook and other sections of northern Maine.

When only about seven years of age, I began using, or abusing, a rifle. At ten I killed my first deer, a grand, glorious and seldom duplicated feeling! Four years later, I got my first wallop at "an old bull"—only a crotch-horn, to be sure, but a bull just the same. From then until I was twenty-seven years old, I killed around a dozen good bulls: some poor, some fair, and some good heads, but never that much-sought-for "god-roncher."

There were some good-sized timber crashers in that baker's dozen, but never one with enough bone north of his forehead to suit me. I wanted one that would make a pasture cedar resemble an under nourished geranium bush in comparison.

The nearest to filling the bill was one I sprayed with a .35 Remington automatic on a beech ridge in the old Skiticook country in 1910. He was there with the "heft," weighing eight hundred pounds on McGary Brothers scales, when we brought him in to Houlton three days later. He was big enough in body, but had a fair head, ten points I think.

However, a few years later, I was destined to meet "The Bull Of My Dreams." While working in Van Buren, on Aroostook's northern border, just across the river from St. Leonards, New Brunswick, I became acquainted with the late Charles L. Cyr of that place. He was an enthusiastic outdoorsman and one of the finest sportsmen I ever met.

Many were the delightful fishing trips we had together on the Tobique, Restigouche and Green River watersheds. We whipped, or rather, he whipped and I lashed, some fine trout waters together.

As we both liked hunting as well as we did fishing, which is saying a lot, it was only natural that, "between bites," our talk would every so often run to guns, deer, bear and bulls; most often "bull," as that mythical one with the big head, that I'd never yet met, was still my obsession.

Perhaps Charley had not shot any more in number than I had, but the heads he had killed were very much larger. In fact, he had one or two of his mounted specimens in his pretty little Hotel Cyr that would just about answer my ideal of a "god-roncher." I remember there were two heads, each with at least twenty points, with an approximate five-foot spread, just magnificent types of the lordly old bull. Every time I'd go into the hotel and look reverently up at those old babies, the valves of my heart would skip like an inadequately lubricated Model T.

Most of Charley's big heads had been killed in the Wild Goose Lake region, on the headwaters of the Green River, forty-five miles north of its junction with the St. John.

His arguments, continued awe-full gazing at those bodiless behemoths, and my life-long ambition to shoot a bull with a really big head, finally decided me to spend my annual two weeks vacation with Charley in that wonderful moose country, Wild Goose Lake and Green River.

Finances, then as now, were scarce, flitting and elusive, but I decided by bumming as much as possible on good-old Charley, that I could afford the trip into this moose-hunter's Mecca.

My rifle was not of as heavy a caliber as I would have chosen for a trip of this nature, but I could not afford a new one, so decided to make do. It was a .30 Remington pump action. That was before the advent of the improved ammunition for the .30-30 and .30 Remington that now develop over 1850 pounds of muzzle energy. But I had cleanly killed several bull moose in the Maine woods with .30-30 and .32 Special guns, and I didn't anticipate that New Brunswick moose were any more reluctant about passing into eternity than their Aroostook brothers. I resolved that I wouldn't strain the gun barrel by attempting any long shots on the lakes or river and, as it worked out, the little Remington was decidedly adequate.

We had our choice of two methods of getting into the Wild Goose Lake region: either by poling canoes up Green River, a distance or forty-five miles, or driving to St. Rose, P.Q., hiring two tote-teams to haul our food, luggage and two canoes through the Temiscouata and Touladi lakes country, and hitting Green River, near its source, on Fourth Lake.

The tote-team method mustered the most votes. It took three days through almost primeval forest until we crossed back into the Province of New Brunswick and hit the foot of Fourth Lake, where we pitched our tent for a ten-day search, if necessary, for the tall, homely, antlered gentleman with the prehensile upper lip.

Teams and teamsters were sent back. Charley had invited, for the trip, a friend of his from Grand Falls, New Brunswick, Laurent Parent. Charles, Mr. Parent and I made up the hunters. We had Joe Russell of St. Jacques, N.B., for a guide. Joe had either hunted or trapped for almost all of that vast wilderness, and he knew of lily-pad infested waters that were otherwise known only to bull frogs and bull moose, as he later proved.

The first night in camp we held a council of war. Charley was particularly anxious that I should get a shot at a big bull and so fulfill his claims made for this, his favorite hunting section.

Of course I was powerful enthusiastic, but not very optimistic. Twenty-odd years of hunting had thoroughly educated me to the fact that it is a mighty uncertain pastime. I did hope and expect that I would get a shot of some sort of a "killable" bull before the trip ended, but bull moose are a mighty scarce commodity at times, and big bulls are always scarce. Hadn't I lived among, chase and killed the old chin-whiskered devils for years and yet never had seen a really good head?

It was Charley's idea that we would probably be obliged to hike to Wild Goose Lake if we sighted a monarch worthwhile. This would entail a nine-mile hike, over nothing more than a spotted trail, and toting a canoe on our shoulders in the bargain, Joe disagreed with Charles' diagnosis. He allowed he knew of a small lake, less than five miles from where we could paddle a canoe, that darned few white men frequented, but was a veritable "factory" for the palmated gentlemen. He said it was called "Belani Lake." If I had not had a world of respect for Joe's knowledge of that country, I would have said it sounded a lot like "baloney," but I refrained.

Daylight the next morning saw the bold Joe and my huge, five-foot-five form climbing out of the canoe, three miles down the lake from our camp. There was no trail, to say nothing of a road, to our destination; only Joe's knowledge of the country, gained in trapping, five years previous. He hit out east, followed a little brook to its source, climbed a mountain, down the other side, through every kind of growth known to our north woods, and about ten in the forenoon, we came out on the shore of Belani Lake!

If I live to be as old as Rabbit Maranville, I'll never forget Belani Lake as it looked that morning. It wasn't a lake, just a pond, but it had all the fixings of a moose's dining room: lily-pads, willows, alders and what-have-you. There were none of the bellowing brethren in sight, but they had all been there, and right recently, too; papa, mamma and the baby, Uncle Joe and all the relatives from over the ridge. The darned place was actually muddy and roily, where they had just left. Trees and bushes all around the entire shore were hooked and broken, and there were places dug a foot deep, where the conceited old males had been throwing mud, for the edification of their lady loves and to intimidate their brethren.

With high hopes and hearts a-pattering, we found a good lookout spot and sat down, hoping that sometime during the day, one of the amorously inclined old boys with the cloven hoofs would amble out.

We stayed there until after twelve o'clock and no sight of moose. Although it was only the first day of October, there was a raw cold wind snapping at us. Then, too, I was getting just a bit impatient. I'm not the best still-hunter in the world; I would rather be on the move doing something, even if it isn't so bright.

Sensing my impatience, Joe informed me that he knew of another little lake about two miles farther on, so we set out for that one. He was ahead, with his little belt ax in his hand, trying to pick out the faint old spots he had made several years before. New Brunswick guides were not allowed to carry guns, but apparently, from force of habit, that little ax was seldom out of Joe's hand. Foliage was thick, as hardly a leaf had fallen.

We had gone probably a mile from Belani Lake, through a hardwood ridge country, when suddenly I saw Joe stop and drop his ax. I followed his gaze and spied an old cow moose making a pretty fast exit, but saw nothing in her appearance to make the taciturn Joe let go of his favorite belt weapon. The next instant I heard a crash, slightly to the left, and looking, caught a flash of a bull's horn and the hazy outline of his form tearing down the ridge. The leaves made visibility darned low, but I had seen enough to know that a bull moose with some bone above his ears was fast leaving for another country, so I snapped into action.

Whatever faults the Remington pump-action rifle may have, slowness is not one. A fellow can hold the butt to his shoulder and sure spray the atmosphere, *when occasion demands. This was one of those occasions! I rattled five shots in the direction where I thought they'd do the most good. The bull was now out of sight.*

In fact, he had never really been in my sight, although I learned later that Joe, who was ahead, had been blessed with a beautiful view of the old baby.

When I ceased the bombardment and looked at Joe, he sure was one excited Frenchman. He allowed that I had a bull and that he was "on old dammer." I felt pretty sure that I had hit the bull several times, but I had seen nothing to make me think he was a very big one.

Joe hunted around and found his ax where he had thrown it; I filled up the magazine with some more .30-30 fodder, and we started over in the general direction where we had last seen and heard the old bull crashing. I confidently expected to find a dead bull and that he would be a fair specimen. Holy Swill! He went less than one hundred yards from where I'd done the shooting when I saw a big black hulk of a body and a mass of horn sticking up toward the zenith, that fairly made my hair curl!

The "god-roncher!" The bull of my dreams! My short legs made a start that would have given Charley Paddock the appearance of being club-footed. That was a golden moment, when I got a close-up of his really splendid head. He had twenty-two points, eleven on a side, including a dandy mass of long brow points; webs almost a foot wide and a bell or chin whisker over fifteen inches long. It was a fine specimen of a bull moose; not a record, but a lot larger than the average.

That is what could be termed real "bull-luck," finding a big fellow in the middle of the day, fully a mile from any water, right in the heart of the thick, green woods; shooting him, the first one sighted on the trip, and such a nice prize.

Two days later, Charley and Parent, not having seen any bulls, started for Belani Lake and the scene of my lucky break. It was only about 8 a.m. when they hit the shore of the little lake. Hardly had they looked the place over when they heard a bull smashing and bellowing on the west side of the lake. His boastings were promptly answered by another old Lothario on the opposite shore. In just a few minutes, the first bull came into view. He was a magnificent sight as he stood on the very edge of the lake, hooking and bawling fighting talk at the other old baby on the opposite shore. This last one did not come out in sight so the boys could see which was the larger, so finally Charley trained his Remington .35 automatic on the first bull, who speedily passed into bull heaven.

This proved to be a fine trophy, with sixteen points and a good web. He had a spread of about fifty inches, but looked small when lined up with mine, which spread a half-inch short of five feet.

We spent a glorious week, taking care of our heads, shooting partridge, catching whitefish, some of which weighed three and four pounds, and looking over other moose which came out on the shores of Fourth and Fifth Lakes. Joe made a trip over to Wilde Goose Lake and reported seeing a bull that was fully as good if not a better head than mine. Some country!

MOOSE HUNTING

We finally loaded our two canoes for the seventy-mile trip down Green River and the St. John to Van Buren. We made it in two days. When I'd get a bit tired swinging the paddle, all I had to do to recoup was to reach back and shut my hand tight on one of the old bull's antlers and I was good for another two hours of hard digging.

That was one of my finest trips in thirty years of hunting. Charley Cyr, the royal companion who made the trip possible, has since died, being killed by a freight train when he was returning from one of the hunting trips which he loved so well. ■

21
DELICIOUS MOOSE RECIPES

his book would not be complete without a chapter that includes a baker's dozen of delicious moose recipes. Although I have had the culinary pleasure and good fortune to have had wild game prepared for me by professional sous-chefs, guides, outfitter's chefs, friends, and my extended family, some of the finest game dishes I have eaten have been prepared by my wife, Kate.

Kate Fiduccia is the segment host of "Cooking Wild in Kate's Kitchen" and the senior editor of Woods N' Water TV Series. She is a graduate of Cornell University's Hotel School with a bachelor's in Business and Hotel Management. Kate has authored several books, *Cooking Wild in Kate's Kitchen, Cooking Wild in Kate's Camp, Grillin' & Chili'n', Backyard Grilling*, and *The Quotable Wine Lover*. Kate is currently writing a cookbook called The Jerky Bible. She also provides wild game cooking demonstrations at many sport shows and big box stores across the country.

Kate has also appeared on the CBS Evening News and MSNBC's News with Brian Williams and was featured in both the *New York Times* and *Newsday* as "the original" female big-game hunter on television.

Here are a few tips from Kate that will enhance the flavor of your moose or any other wild game you prepare.

- Young game provides the most tender and tasteful meat.
- The best flavor will come from an animal that was killed quickly.
- The quicker an animal is field-dressed *properly,* the better table-fare its meat will be.
- The faster the hide is removed the better the flavor of the meat will be.
- Don't hang game outdoors for long periods, particularly when temperatures rise and fall.
- Cured meat only occurs when meat is hung in coolers with temperatures of thirty-seven to forty-one degrees.

Kate hopes you will enjoy her moose recipes in this chapter. You can visit www.woodsnwater.tv for additional wild game recipes, books, and Kate's game steakhouse and Asian sauces.

MOOSE FILET WITH MORSELS

Every time I take any big-game animal (especially moose), I remove the tenderloin as quickly as possible. Even though I have been doing this for years, I find that each time I am removing the tenderloins, I am always planning in my head how I will cook this choicest of all cuts. One way to enhance tenderloins to its max is with this recipe!

Serves 6 to 8
Cooking time: under 30 minutes

1 cup butter (2 sticks), divided
2 tablespoons pepper
2 pounds venison tenderloin, cut into
½-inch-thick medallions
1 cup plus 2 teaspoons all-purpose
flour, divided
12 ounces fresh morel mushrooms,
chopped
½ cup sherry
2 tablespoons freshly chopped chives or
wild onion tops
²/₃ cup beef broth
Salt and pepper

In Dutch oven, heat one stick of the butter over medium-high heat until sizzling. Press the pepper into the loin steaks and then dip them into the ½ cup flour. Add to hot butter and sauté until just browned on both sides. Take care not to overcook the venison from Dutch oven and keep warm.

Add remaining butter, mushrooms, sherry, and chives to Dutch oven. Cook for 5 to 7 minutes, or until morels are tender. Meanwhile, combine remaining 2 teaspoons flour and beef broth in small bowl, stirring to blend and remove any lumps. When mushrooms are tender, add broth mixture, stirring constantly. Cook, stirring constantly, until sauce thickens. Season sauce with salt and pepper to taste. Divide venison steaks between plates and top with mushroom sauce.

EASY VENISON GOULASH

You may substitute a less-tender cut of venison for the loin steak in this recipe; simply simmer if for about an hour before adding the beans.

Serves 2
Cooking time: 30 to 60 minutes

1 tablespoon vegetable oil
10 ounces moose sirloin steak, cut into ½-inch cubes
½ cup all-purpose flour, plus a little more to thicken sauce
2 medium onions, chopped
1 single-serve package dry tomato soup mix
¾ cup water
1 (8-ounce) can red kidney beans, drained
Salt and pepper
Hot cooked rice or noodles for serving, optional

In large skillet or Dutch oven, heat oil over medium-high heat. Coat venison cubes with flour, shaking to remove excess. Add venison to skillet and brown on all sides. Add onions, soup mix, and water. Reduce heat and simmer for about 30 minutes. Add beans; cook for 10 minutes longer. Season to taste with salt and pepper. If mixture is too watery, add a little flour to thicken. Serve over hot rice or noodles.

BAKED ZITI WITH MOOSE

A loaf of savory Italian garlic bread makes a great accompaniment to this dish. If you have cooked ziti on hand, preparation time is reduced to 10 minutes . . . quick and easy!

Serves 4
Prep time: 25 minutes
Cooking time: 35 minutes

8 ounces uncooked ziti pasta
½ cup finely chopped onion
3 cloves garlic, minced
2 tablespoons canola oil
1 cup chopped broccoli
1 pound ground moose meat
½ teaspoon crumbled dried oregano
½ teaspoon salt
¼ teaspoon black pepper
¼ teaspoon hot red pepper flakes
1 (8-ounce) can tomato sauce
1 cup canned mushrooms, undrained
2 cups shredded mozzarella cheese
½ cup grated Parmesan cheese

Heat oven to 350°F. Prepare ziti according to package directions. Drain; set aside.

In large skillet, sauté onion and garlic in oil over medium-high heat until softened; do not let garlic brown. Add broccoli and sauté for 3 to 5 minutes longer. Add venison, oregano, salt, black pepper, and red pepper flakes. Cook until venison is no longer pink, stirring to break up meat. Mix in tomato sauce and mushrooms with their liquid. Heat to a simmer. Add cooked ziti and mix well. Transfer mixture to shallow casserole. Sprinkle both cheeses on top and bake, uncovered, for 35 minutes, or until mixture bubbles and cheese is lightly browned.

MOOSE TAMALE PIE

Here's a dish that takes a little bit of extra time because of the cornmeal crust. But it's worth the effort!

Serves 6
Prep time: 20 minutes
Cooking time: 40 minutes

Filling
1 tablespoon canola oil
1 pound ground venison
4 scallions, chopped
1 (8-ounce) can tomato sauce
1 cup whole-kernel corn, drained
¼ cup chopped Anaheim peppers (for more zing, use a blend of Anaheim and jalapeno peppers)
¼ cup evaporated milk
¼ cup cornmeal
1 teaspoon chili powder
1 teaspoon salt
½ teaspoon pepper
½ teaspoon cumin
¼ teaspoon crumbled dried oregano leaves

Cornmeal Pie Crust
1 cup all-purpose flour, plus additional for rolling out crust
2 tablespoons cornmeal
⅓ cup vegetable shortening
3 to 4 tablespoons cold water

Topping
1 egg, lightly beaten
½ teaspoon dry mustard
1 cup shredded Monterey Jack cheese
1 cup shredded cheddar cheese
6 pitted black olives, sliced
Sour cream and chopped tomatoes for garnish, optional

Heat oven to 425°F.

To prepare filling: In large skillet, heat oil over medium heat. Add venison and cook until no longer pink, stirring to break up. Drain. Mix in remaining filling ingredients. Let simmer for 5 minutes, then remove from the heat.

To prepare crust: In a small bowl, blend together flour and cornmeal. Cut in shortening with pastry blender or two knives. When mixture resembles coarse meal or very small peas, add water a little at a time, mixing with fork until dough forms. Roll out pastry on a floured surface until it forms a 15-inch circle. Fit pastry into deep-dish 9-inch pie pan and crimp edges.

Spoon filling into pie crust. Place pie pan on baking sheet and bake for 25 minutes. While it is baking, prepare the topping for the pie. Combine egg, milk, and mustard in medium bowl; mix well. When pie has baked for 25 minutes, remove from oven, sprinkle cheeses over filling, and pour milk mixture on top. Decorate with sliced olives. Return to oven and bake for an additional 5 minutes. Let stand for 10 minutes before serving. Serve with sour cream and chopped tomatoes.

MOOSE MEATBALL STEW

I remember one particularly severe winter here on the East Coast. By early February, we were hit by our thirteenth official snowstorm of the season. During this particular sweetheart's month, Peter spent plenty of time outside plowing the driveway and clearing snow off the outbuilding, cars, and ornamental shrubbery. I spent much of the time inside keeping one eye on him, the other on our young son, Cody, and preparing savory, warm venison meals from both deer and moose. One of my sweetheart's favorite meals is venison meatball stew. Even though the meatballs and vegetables are hearty and savory, it's knowing how good a piece of buttered Italian bread will taste after it has been dunked into the sauce that puts this recipe on my "A" list. Enjoy!

Serves 4
Prep Time: 40 minutes
Cooking Time: 45 minutes

For the Meatballs
1 pound ground venison
¾ cup Italian-seasoned bread crumbs
2 tablespoons chopped fresh parsley
1 teaspoon minced garlic
¼ teaspoon pepper
1 egg, lightly beaten
Olive oil as needed

For the Stew
1 tablespoon olive oil
½ cup chopped onion
½ cup chopped green bell peppers
½ teaspoon chopped garlic
1 teaspoon salt
1 (14.5-ounce) can plum tomatoes, undrained
2 (8-ounce) cans tomato sauce
¼ teaspoon crumbled dried oregano
¼ teaspoon cumin
¼ teaspoon pepper

¾ pound zucchini, peeled and sliced into ½-inch-thick rounds
½ pound carrots, sliced in ⅛-inch-thick rounds
Hot cooked rice or egg noodles for serving, optional

First, make the meatballs. In a mixing bowl, combine all meatball ingredients except oil. Mix thoroughly and shape into meatballs about 1 inch in diameter. Heat a small amount of oil in a large heavy-bottom skillet over medium-high heat. Brown meatballs on all sides and transfer to a bowl.

Now start preparing the rest of the stew. In a stockpot or Dutch oven, heat the tablespoon of oil over medium heat. Add onions, green peppers, and garlic and sauté until softened. Stir in tomatoes with their juices, tomato sauce, oregano, cumin, and pepper. Heat to a slow simmer. Add zucchini and carrots; cover and simmer for about 15 minutes.

Add browned meatballs to pot; cover and cook for 20 to 30 minutes longer. Serve with white rice or egg noodles.

MOOSE STEW WITH BARLEY

Since this stew is prepared in a skillet, make sure you have one that's large enough—at least twelve inches in diameter. The aroma while this stew is cooking will have you fighting back hungry ones until it's time to eat!

Serves 4
Prep time: 30 minutes
Cooking time: 2 hours

½ pound pearl onions*
9 large fresh shiitake mushrooms, stems removed and discarded (½- to ¾-pound white mushrooms may be substituted)
2 cups peeled, cubed butternut squash (1-inch cubes)
1 tablespoon canola oil
1¼ teaspoon crumbled dried thyme, divided
1½ pounds boneless moose shoulder or rump, cut into 1-inch cubes, all connective tissue removed
Seasoned pepper (such as McCormick's California Style Blend Garlic Pepper)
3 cups beef stock or canned unsalted beef broth
1 bay leaf
1 large clove garlic, minced
¾ cup pearl barley
Water as needed (approx. ¾ cup)
Chopped fresh parsley for garnish

*You can use thawed frozen pearl onions in place of fresh if you'd like; it'll save you some time, as you won't need to boil and peel them.

Heat large saucepan of water to boiling. Add pearl onions and boil for 2 to 3 minutes to loosen skins. Drain and cool slightly. Cut off root ends. Squeeze onions from stem end; the onions will slip out of their skins. Place onions in large bowl.

Cut mushroom caps into halves (white mushrooms may be halved or left whole, depending on size). Add mushrooms, squash, oil, and 1 teaspoon of the thyme to the bowl with onions, stirring gently to coat vegetables. Heat large non-stick skillet over high heat. Add vegetables and sauté until browned. Use slotted spoon to return vegetables to bowl; set aside.

Sprinkle venison with seasoned pepper. Brown seasoned venison cubes in small batches and transfer to a plate. When all venison is browned, return to skillet. Add beef stock, bay leaf, garlic, and remaining ¼ teaspoon thyme. Heat to boiling. Reduce heat, cover, and simmer for 15 minutes. Stir in barley. Cover and simmer for 45 minutes. Stir vegetables into stew. Cover and simmer until vegetables and barley are tender, about 45 minutes longer; add water as needed during cooking to keep mixture moist. Remove bay leaf. Sprinkle stew with parsley and serve.

VENISON VEGETABLE FRITTATA

Frittatas are ideal dishes for spring and summer because they're light and they cook quickly. I tasted my first frittata at a Mama Lucci's restaurant in the Little Italy section of New York City many years ago. It was a hot summer's day, and the lunchtime crowd had packed the air-conditioned bistros. Peter and I decided to take a sidewalk seat instead and do the "New York" thing—people-watching while enjoying a light meal.

I started making this dish a few years ago to change up our summer brunches. It's perfect when we've had an early rise to start working in the yard and have skipped a good breakfast. Serve it with a side of salsa and fresh-baked biscuits.

Serves 6
Prep time: 15 minutes
Cooking time: 30 minutes

½ pound ground moose meat
Salt, black pepper, and cayenne pepper
$1^2/_5$ cup unsalted butter, divided
3 tablespoons minced shallots
1 tablespoon minced garlic
1 pound fresh button mushrooms, sliced
½ cup diced fresh zucchini
8 eggs, room temperature
½ pound fresh spinach leaves, torn or finely chopped
1 cup small-curd cottage cheese
¼ cup grated Parmesan cheese
1 tablespoon olive oil

Cook ground moose meat in large skillet over medium heat until no longer pink, stirring to break up. Season to taste with salt, black pepper, and cayenne pepper; set aside.

In large omelet pan (minimum 12 inches), melt 2 tablespoons of the butter over medium heat. Add shallots and garlic and cook for about 3 minutes. Add mushrooms and zucchini. Sauté until liquid from the mushrooms has evaporated. Remove from heat and set aside to cool.

Heat broiler. Beat eggs in large bowl. Mix spinach, cottage cheese, and cooled venison mixture. Add the cooled mushroom mixture and stir until well combined.

Set omelet pan over medium-high heat. Melt remaining 2 tablespoons butter. Add egg mixture; as it begins to set, shake the pan to ensure it does not stick. Turn heat to low. Without stirring, continue cooking for about 10 minutes, checking to make sure the eggs do not stick to the pan.

When egg mixture is almost completely set, sprinkle Parmesan cheese and drizzle oil on top of the frittata. Place pan under the broiler to melt cheese; be careful not to over-cook. Slide frittata onto serving platter; cut into 6 portions.

ASIAN VENISON LETTUCE WRAPS

Serving size: 10–12 leaf portions
Prep time: 20 minutes
Cooking time: 20 minutes

3 tablespoons sesame oil
1½ pound ground moose venison
1 teaspoon garlic powder
1 cup mushrooms, minced
1 cup water chestnuts (8-ounce can), minced
¼ cup onions, minced
2 tablespoons hoisin sauce
¼ cup Kate's Asian Grill Sauce (or any soy-based sauce)
Lettuce leaves (preferably Boston Bibb)
Chinese mustard

Heat a large sauté pan over medium heat. Add 1 tablespoon sesame oil to warm slightly. Add in the ground venison and cook until it is no longer pink. While it is cooking, sprinkle with garlic powder. When the meat is browned, remove it from the pan. Do not drain. Let it cool slightly.

Combine the cooked venison, mushrooms, water chestnuts, and minced onions in a bowl. Return empty pan to medium heat. Add 2 tbsp. sesame oil and add in venison mixture. Season with hoisin sauce and Kate's Asian Grill sauce. Mix well to let all flavors blend together. Serve in lettuce leaves and top each portion with a bit of Chinese mustard.

SAN ANTONIO VENISON CABBAGE DIP

Serves 6
Prep time: 15 minutes
Cooking time: 20–30 minutes

1 pound ground moose venison
1 pound uncooked bacon, chopped
1 small head red cabbage, chopped into small bits
1 jalapeño pepper, minced
1 large (24-ounce) jar salsa
1 teaspoon chili powder
Corn tortilla chips for serving

Cook ground moose venison in a large skillet over medium heat until no longer pink, stirring to break up. Drain and set aside. In another large skillet, cook bacon until crispy. Use slotted spook to transfer bacon to paper towel-lined plate: set aside. Add cabbage and jalapeño pepper to bacon grease in skillet and cook over medium heat until cabbage softens. Add salsa, chili powder, cooked venison, and bacon to the skillet. Stir to mix thoroughly, and cook until heated through. Remove from heat and serve with corn tortilla chips.

BOURSIN STEAKHOUSE VENISON POCKETS

Serves 4
Prep time: 45 minutes
Cooking time: 10–15 minutes

1–1½ pounds venison loin steak, thin
¼ cup Kate's Gourmet Steakhouse Grill Sauce, or a steakhouse sauce of your choice
One medium onion, sliced
4 ounces Boursin cheese (herbed cream cheese)
2 large pita pockets, halved

Place the venison and the Steakhouse Grill Sauce in a zip-top bag and let marinate about 30 minutes. Preheat the grill for about 20 minutes. The grill should be hot enough that you can hold your hand over it for only a few seconds.

Place the onions slices on the grill. To make sure the slices do not fall through the grates, you can place them in a hinged basket. Cook until they are browned on both sides. Place the steaks on the grill and cook for about 1 to 2 minutes each side, depending upon the thickness of the steak. Remove when it is medium rare. Cut into slices and set aside. Spread Boursin cheese on the inside of each of the pita pockets. Place a slice of grilled onion and some sliced steak inside the pocket. Repeat for the remaining pockets. Place the assembled pita pockets on the grill and heat for about 30 seconds each side. Serve immediately. Side accompaniments may include sour cream, salsa, guacamole, chopped black olives, or sliced jalapeños.

POPCORN VENISON

Serves 4 (as a snack)
Prep time: 20–30 minutes
Cooking time: 15 minutes

Peanut oil (to fill line in deep fryer or about 2 inches deep in a stove pot)
1½ cups flour
1½ cups buttermilk
1½ cups breadcrumbs, seasoned
1 pound venison loin or steak, cut in bite-size pieces

Heat peanut oil in deep fryer. If you do not have a deep fryer, add peanut oil to about 2 inches high—enough to cover the venison pieces. Heat to about 350 to 370 degrees. Place the flour, buttermilk, and breadcrumbs each in separate bowls. Dredge some venison bits in the flour; then soak in buttermilk and then coat with the breadcrumbs. Place several pieces in the hot oil and cook for about 2 minutes. Remove from oil with slotted spoon and place on paper-towel lined plate. Poke each piece with a toothpick and serve with a dip or just plain!

GARLIC-LIME MOOSE STEAK

This is one that was derived from a recipe that was shared with me by a college friend named Sylvia. Sylvia was from Cuba and loved to share with us some of her native recipes during the seemingly endless winter months in upstate New York. I later adapted this flavorful one for moose steak.

Serves 4
Prep time: 15 minutes
Cooking time: 10 minutes

Garlic-Lime Rub:
1 teaspoon kosher salt
½ teaspoon freshly ground black pepper
6 cloves garlic, minced
½ teaspoon cumin
⅛ teaspoon ground cayenne pepper
½ cup fresh lime juice
2 tablespoons olive oil

In a mortar, combine the salt, pepper, garlic, cumin, and ground cayenne pepper. Grind the ingredients to a paste. Slowly drizzle in the lime juice and olive oil, alternately, until it has reached a smooth consistency.

Steaks

4 small moose steaks, trimmed of all connective tissue and fat, 6 to 8 ounces each

1 pound Portobello mushrooms, sliced ¼-inch thick

2 tablespoons olive oil

salt to taste

Place the venison steaks in a glass baking dish and, with a pastry brush, lightly coat both sides of the steaks with the garlic-lime rub. Let sit for 15 to 20 minutes.

While the steaks sit, preheat the grill for about twenty minutes. The grill should be hot enough that you can hold your hand over it for only a few seconds.

Place the mushrooms in a bowl and drizzle with olive oil and a little salt. Toss to coat. Place the mushrooms in an oiled, long-handled, hinged, grill basket. Set on the grill to cook in a cooler section of the grill.

Place the steaks in the center of the grill. Grill about two minutes each side, while basting with the rub. Grill the mushrooms about two to three minutes per side, seasoning with salt and pepper.

Transfer the steaks to plates, let sit for a few minutes. Serve with the grilled mushrooms on the side.

GRILLED MOOSE WELLINGTON

In my first venison cookbook I shared my recipe for the classic Venison Wellington that is baked in the oven. This twist on that classic is one of my fancier preparations for the grill. It's sure to please any guest.

Serves 4

Prep time: 20 minutes

Cooking time: 20 minutes

4 moose loin medallions, about 1½ inches thick, trimmed free of all fat and connective tissue

2 tablespoons olive oil

salt and freshly ground black pepper to taste

4 large Portobello mushroom caps

4 large slices Italian bread, ½-inch thick

3 cups brown sauce

⅓ cup duck liver pate, room temperature

Preheat the grill for about twenty minutes. The grill should be hot enough so that you can hold your hand over it for only a few seconds.

Brush the medallions with the oil and season with salt and pepper. Brush the portobellos with oil and season with salt and pepper.

Lightly oil the grill plate before placing the medallions on the grill. Cook over high heat until they are seared on both sides (1 to 2 minutes). Move to a cooler part of the grill to continue cooking, turning occasionally. Cook until the internal temperature is 125°F (medium-rare). Remove from the grill and let them sit for 5 minutes to let the juices set.

Grill the mushrooms until seared on both sides. Set aside and keep warm.

On a cooler section of the grill, lightly toast the Italian bread slices on both sides.

Heat the brown sauce in a small sauce pan. Spread about 1 tablespoon of the pate on each slice of toasted bread. Slice the mushrooms and arrange them on top of the pate. Slice the medallions into ¼-inch thick strips and layer them on top of the mushroom slices.

Drizzle the brown sauce across the moose medallions and serve warm.

Acknowledgments

I need to thank Maryo Pepin, the employees, and pro-staff at Buck Expert Research Center for always being willing to share information.

Bernard Metivier, while you speak French and I speak English, thanks for teaching me the language of the moose.

To all the guides that I have worked with over he years: Ron Piccard, Rick Dodge, George Perry, Roger Avery, and Dan Glidden; the days and nights in moose camp along with the stories and hunts we all shared inspired this book.

To all the hunters I have guided over the years, thank you! I relive all of those hunts from time to time and I had a great time with all of you. I hope you did too.

To all who contributed pictures to this book–Roger Stevens, Maryo Pepin, Rick Dodge, Bernard Metivier, and everyone else, thanks! Words only go so far.